In Loving Memory:
A Tribute to Tim Horton

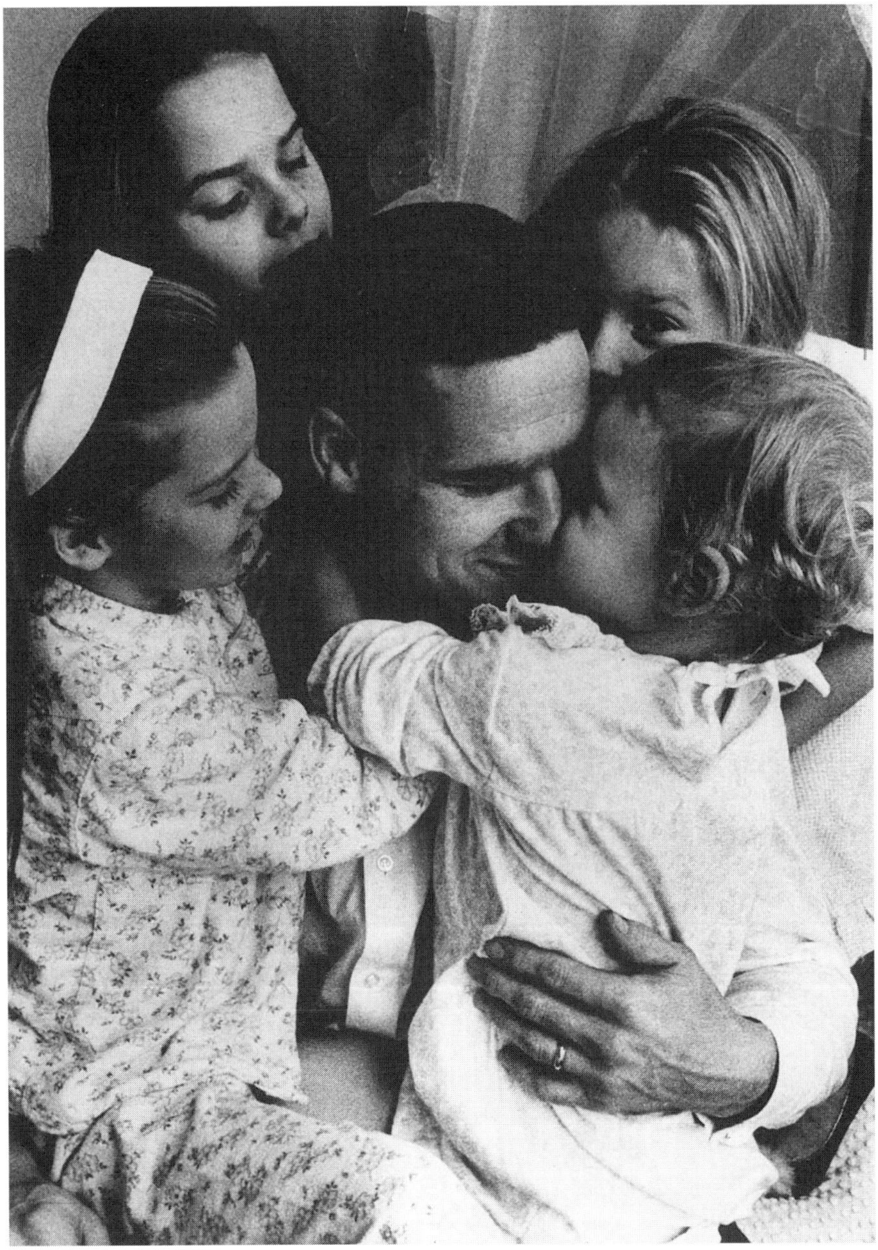

In Loving Memory

A TRIBUTE TO

TIM HORTON

by LORI HORTON
and TIM GRIGGS

God Bless
Lori Horton

To Pete march/96
Best wishes T Griggs

ECW PRESS

Front cover photo reproduced courtesy Graphic Artists/Hockey Hall of
Fame. Back cover action photo courtesy Frank Prazak/Hockey Hall of Fame.
Frontispiece photo by Frank Lennon; back page photo courtesy John Subura.
All other photos, unless otherwise credited, are from the authors' collection.

CANADIAN CATALOGUING IN PUBLICATION DATA

Griggs, Tim
In loving memory : a tribute to Tim Horton

ISBN 1-55022-319-4

1. Horton, Tim, 1930–1974. 2. Hockey players –
Canada – Biography. I. Horton, Lori. II. Title.
GV848.5.H58G74 1997   796.962'092   C97-931519-0

Design and imaging by ECW Type & Art, Oakville, Ontario.
Printed by Metropole Litho, Sherbrooke, Quebec.

Distributed in Canada by General Distribution Services,
30 Lesmill Road, Don Mills, Ontario M3B 2T6.

Distributed in the United States by Login Publishers Consortium,
436 West Randolph Street, Chicago, Illinois 60607.

Published by ECW PRESS,
2120 Queen Street East, Suite 200,
Toronto, Ontario M4E 1E2.

http://www.ecw.ca/press

PRINTED AND BOUND IN CANADA

ACKNOWLEDGEMENTS

The authors would like to thank the following people who helped make this book possible:

Tom and Kim Meny; Kelly Horton; Cam, Traci, Tim, and A.J. Simone; Ron Jr., Jeri, and Corey; Joyce, Glen, and Auriol Horton; Joy MacMillan; Irene McCauley; Ab Demarco; Dave Keon; Allan and Barbara Stanley; Bill Gadsby; Larry and Gloria Mann; Frank Mahovlich; Tom Pashby; Dick Duff; Vic Hadfield; Andra and Leonard "Red" Kelly; Eddie and Norma Shack; Joe and Bonnie Crozier; George Armstrong; Johnny Bower; Paul Terbenche; Jim Schoenfeld; Keith McCreary; Bob Baun; Hugh Phillips; Joe, Jim, Jane, and Gord Griggs; Donna and Dennis Griggs; Dini Petty; Steve Connor; Sharon Van Der Ender; Steve Richard.

Father O'Brien at St. Michael's College; Ann at Sudbury High School; Craig Campbell and the rest of the incredibly helpful staff at the Hockey Hall of Fame. Billy Harris, Dennis Miles, Bob Shaver, Bob Paul, and John Subura for their photos and their generosity; Frank Lennon; Randy Foster at Exposed Photos Services.

George Gross, *Open Ice* by Doug Hunter, Billy Harris's *The Glory Years*, Andrew Podnieks and his trusty *Blue and White Book*; our publisher Jack David, our editor, Kevin Connolly, Paul Davies, who designed the book, and the rest of the ECW staff.

For Corey, Tim, A.J., Kylie, and Sean

This is Tim at age 8 or 9 in Cochrane, about 250 miles north of North Bay. Cochrane was a railway terminus but the population when Tim was growing up was only about 2,000.

I

'Thrifty'

The Copper Cliff Redmen put an ad in the paper for tryouts. I decided to try out . . . and I said to Tim, "Why don't you and Ray come?" Tim said, "We won't make that team," and I said, "I know, I won't make it either, but let's just go. The ice isn't going to freeze on the lake — Why don't we just go and try out . . . we'll enjoy it, and we'll at least get some ice time."

— *George Armstrong*

TIM HORTON WAS BORN on a cold Sunday, January 12, 1930, in Lady Minto Hospital in Cochrane, Ontario, a small town about 250 miles north of North Bay. He was the first child of Ethel and Aaron Oakley Horton, and although his mother had named him Tim long before the birth — while she sat sewing and knitting what she referred to as "Timmy's trousseau" — she was too ill to attend the christening, where his father named him Miles Gilbert Horton, after his two grandfathers. No matter; he was always Tim to relatives and friends, and later to his many fans. Except for certain documents and the odd piece of official business, Tim's given names were never used.

Tim's mother was born Ethel Irish in North Bay, and moved to Cochrane in the early 1920s. Aaron Oakley Horton (whom most people called "Oak") met Ethel when he moved to Cochrane looking for work. They married in Belleville, where the Hortons' ancestors, United Empire Loyalists, had settled many years before. The couple soon returned to Cochrane, where they lived through the

Depression years. Work was scarce in those days and Oak scrounged employment wherever he could, doing a variety of jobs. In 1933, Tim's brother Gerry was born. Three years later, the family moved with their father to Duparquet, Quebec, where Oak had found a job at Beattie's gold mine. Returning to Cochrane a few years later, Oak landed a job as a mechanic on the Algoma Central Railroad.

Unfortunately, the job was based in Sault Ste. Marie, and Oak was an absentee father through most of Tim and Gerry's early years. Ethel had her hands full with two boisterous children, but she also had the help of her extended family — Ethel's sister Emma and her husband John, and especially, Tim's Aunt Mamie and Uncle Mel Owens.

The population of Cochrane today is 5,500, but back then it was around 2,000. It's one of those charming Northern Ontario towns, small and friendly. Though circumstances

Tim (on the left) at about age 15, with friends Jerry Stevens and John Fingland (standing).

GLEN MACMILLAN

kept Tim in Toronto for most of his life, he loved the Ontario North. He spoke often of returning there one day. I lived in a large city all my life, and I don't think I could have ever adjusted to living there permanently. It's the −50°c winters that I would object to. But it really is a pretty little town and I would like to visit more often.

Cochrane sits on the edge of Commando Lake, which really appears to be two lakes, surrounded by parkland and some lovely places to walk. The lake freezes in the winter and Tim used to live just up the street. He used to walk down to the lake with his friends and like a lot of Canadian boys they'd clear a spot and play hockey.

Tim at age 16 with his father, Oak, and his dog, Sandy. Quite the physique for a teenager.
DON ROPE

People over the years have wondered why so many great NHL players have come from these small, Northern Ontario towns. It certainly has a lot to do with long, cold winters and an abundance of frozen lakes and rivers. Ice time is never a problem in a town like Cochrane. Tim learned to skate by the age of three, started minor hockey in Duparquet, and continued playing when the family returned to Cochrane. Tim's cousin Ron Owens owned the only hockey puck in town, and was in the habit of taking it home with him whenever he was angry with the other kids. But no matter, the game continued anyway, with a frozen clod of horse manure — what they used to call a "road apple" — serving the purpose just as well.

TIM'S UNCLE MEL managed the outdoor arena in Cochrane, and with Oak away with the railroad, it was Mel who became Tim's hockey mentor. Tim's mother never saw him play a game until he turned professional with the AHL Pittsburgh Hornets some ten years later.

One of Tim's best friends from childhood was Glen Mac-Millan, who still lives in Cochrane with his wife, Joy: "The first time I met Tim was in public school in about grade 4 or 5," MacMillan recalls. "He was a pretty rough and tumble kid. I got into a scrap with him at recess time — I don't remember how it ended — but that's how I met him."

"He was always big on physical fitness. We used to go around the lake and lift rocks, like we were weight-lifting, when we were about 13 or 14. There used to be these big motor oil signs in the old days with a pipe and a big iron base that was about three feet across. Tim and I got a hold of two of these; we kept them at my Dad's place, and we used to lift those too."

"I remember one day my dad came out and said, 'Let me try that,' and he could barely lift one. And Tim and I were only about 13 at that time."

Even as an adult Tim was fairly small — the Leafs' programs listed him at 5'10" but really he was a little under 5'9" — and as a young player never weighed much more than 175 pounds. In his late twenties his weight increased to 185, and while he was well-built and muscular he was only slightly taller than Dick Duff and Dave Keon. I know Tim never told anyone he was five-ten. Back then, though, the players weren't as big as they are now in the NHL, where they all seem to be 6'2" and 220 pounds, so size was never much of an issue for Tim. When you ask them, the one thing people who played with and against him will remember first about Tim was his great strength — even in his forties he was the strongest player on his team. And it all started when he was boy in Cochrane, competing with his friend over who could pick up the biggest rock.

As a child, Tim grew quickly; he was nearly full size by the time he was 10 or 12 years old. Tim was always stronger than the other kids, and he worked all his life to control his temper. Tim's quiet demeanor always made him appear more mild mannered than he was. He had a terrible temper, in fact, but most of the time he controlled it extremely well. In later years Tim admitted to being a childhood bully — he used to beat up on his brother, and his cousin Ron — who's still alive and will attest to that. It was something Tim had a guilt complex about, even as an adult. He started going to church, all by himself, at age 12, in a conscious effort to change his ways. Even at that young age he recognized that spirituality was a necessary part of a well-

4

That's me in the middle with Tim's childhood friend Glen MacMillan, and his wife, Joy. Two of my grandchildren are in front, and in the background is Commando Lake, where Tim learned to skate.

rounded life, and he continued to attend Sunday services throughout his life. I went with him after we were married when he was at home, and I took our daughters so they could benefit from Sunday School, but it was never as important to us as it was for Tim. Even up at the cottage Tim would hop in his boat Sunday morning and go into town for church. When he was playing hockey on the road he'd drag a few of the guys with him — the ones who were Protestants like him.

In addition to being a strong boy, Tim was, as might be expected, a pretty fine hockey player. From the moment he put on skates, Tim was a natural, and it came as no surprise to the kids who grew up with him when Tim made it big in hockey. Cochrane resident David Rudyk remembers playing with Tim on the lake when they were both in elementary school. "He was one of the better hockey players in the whole school. We just couldn't keep up with him. The puck was all his."

Glen MacMillan has much the same memory. "In the winter, we would go down to the lake and clear a big patch of ice so we could play hockey. Even as a little kid Tim was an excellent player; fast with a very good shot."

During the war Tim got a job as a caller at the railway yard — he was 14 at the time. Because Cochrane was a railroad centre, the crews all lived in town. Each morning Tim had to rise before dawn and bicycle through the railway yards

5

This is Tim's worksheet from when he worked as a caller with the railroad in Cochrane. He used to have to get up in the wee hours and bicycle through the railway yards on his way to waking up the morning crews.

TIM HORTON MUSEUM,
COCHRANE

CANADIAN NATIONAL RAILWAYS.-SERVICE RECORD

NAME IN FULL __Timothy Miles Horton   Age 14__ S.R.B. No. _____
PLACE OF BIRTH __Cochrane__ DATE OF BIRTH __Jan 12 1930__ NATIONALITY_____
HEIGHT_____ WEIGHT_____ FORM_____ COMPLEXION_____ COLOR OF HAIR_____ COLOR OF EYES_____
I.'s P.S, OR E.R. & I.A. No._____ CLASS_____ DATE ELIGIBLE FOR PENSION_____
NAME AND ADDRESS OF NEAREST RELATIVE_____

DEPT.	STATION	OCCUPATION	RATE OF PAY	DATE EFFECTIVE	DATE LEFT DEPT.	CAUSE OF LEAVING	STATE WHETHER OR NOT EMPLOYED DURING BREAK IN SERVICE
YD	Cochrane	Caller	41.44	5-10-44	9-1-44	back to	school

RECORD OF NON-APPEARANCE ON PAY ROLLS

OUT OF SERVICE		CAUSE OF NON-APPEARANCE ON PAY ROLLS	OUT OF SERVICE		CAUSE OF NON-APPEARANCE ON PAY ROLLS
FROM (DATE OFF DUTY)	TO (DATE RESUMED DUTY)		FROM (DATE OFF DUTY)	TO (DATE RESUMED DUTY)	

while it was still dark. The railway yards were rather desolate — you'd have to see it to appreciate it — and Tim always had an active imagination. In the cold winter, in the dark, his imagination would work overtime, and he'd nearly scare himself to death, seeing all sorts of things out there as he pedaled past. It was something he could do to himself even when he was older — imagine something terrible and give himself the creeps.

Despite his interest in hockey, like a lot of kids who grew up in Canada during the war, Tim's dream was not to be a hockey player but a fighter pilot. Tim spent hours as a child drawing and building models of Spitfires, the speedy British fighter planes which beat the mighty German Luftwaffe in the Battle of Britain. Still, dreams of a hockey career couldn't have lagged too far back in his mind — in later years the best day Tim could remember from childhood was his sixth birthday, the day his aunt Evelyn Irish presented him with a complete Maple Leaf uniform.

In 1945, Oak Horton took a job with the CPR in Sudbury, so the family pulled up stakes and moved to a house on McLeod Street in Gatchell, in the southwest quarter of Sudbury. But Tim never lost touch with his roots in Cochrane; he kept in close touch with friends and relatives there long after he'd moved on to Toronto, and eventually, New York and Buffalo. And Tim's Aunt Mamie received a dozen red roses every Christmas from her nephew, wherever he was, for the rest of her life. I remember Tim telling me more than once that he thought every child should have a Cochrane to grow up in.

Tim's school in Cochrane. Tim went to public school here before moving on to Sudbury High School.

TIM HAD ALREADY crossed paths with a kid named Dave Keon while playing minor hockey in Duparquet, but his coincidental meetings with future teammates really started on McLeod Street. There the Hortons lived literally across the street from a pint-sized Eddie Shack (who soon became one of Gerry's buddies), and at Sudbury High School, Tim befriended a teenaged George Armstrong, the legendary Maple Leaf star and long-time captain of the team. Armstrong proved to be instrumental in launching Tim's hockey career, but, of course, neither could have dreamed of the glory they would share years later as teammates on four Stanley Cup winners in Toronto, or that they would both one day be inducted into the Hockey Hall of Fame.

"There was Red McCarthy, Tim, and myself," Armstrong remembers. "We played together on the Sudbury High School team, and a fellow named Charlie Cerre was the coach. Cerre came down to St. Michael's College a few years later as well, but Tim already knew him quite well from Sudbury. Tim played football as well as hockey, but I lived in Falconbridge, and my bus used to leave at 4:15 p.m., so all I could do with football was kick, and then I'd have to catch the bus."

"Anyway, the way we got started was this. In grade 10

7

there were four of us from the Sudbury High School team — Dick Trainor, Red McCarthy, Tim and myself. It was October, coming around to the time of the year when the Copper Cliff Redmen, a Junior A team, put an ad in the paper for tryouts. I decided to try out for the team and so I said to Tim, 'Why don't you and Ray come?' And Tim said, 'We won't make that team,' and I said, 'I know, I won't make it either, but let's just go. The lake isn't going to freeze so

The 1946 Sudbury High School junior hockey team. Tim is third from the left in the back row, next to coach Charlie Cerre. Tim's pal "Red" McCarthy is just below him in the front row.

THE WOLF HOWL, YEARBOOK, 1946

we're not going to get ice for a long time. Why don't we just go and try out, we've got nothing to lose. We'll enjoy it and we'll at least get the ice time.' So Red, Tim and I decided to go and, sure enough, didn't the three of us make the team!"

When George decided to quit school in the eleventh grade, he set in motion a process that brought Tim to Toronto to play for St. Michael's College, and eventually, found them both playing for the Maple Leafs.

"When I signed with the Maple Leafs," Armstrong recalls, "the same scout who signed me, a fellow by the name of Bob Wilson, was also very interested in Tim, but he was dubious about Tim's eyesight. In those days they didn't

8

Tim also played rugby in high school (he's second from the left in the back row). Tim's teammate Red McCarthy insisted that he could easily have ended up as "a great halfback" somewhere if it hadn't worked out in hockey.

THE WOLF HOWL, YEARBOOK, 1946

know you could fit people up with contact lenses. Wilson wouldn't have known about that."

In the final game of the Northern Ontario Hockey Association junior finals Tim fell into the boards heavily during the second period. With Bob Wilson watching, Tim had to be helped off the ice. X-rays revealed a broken ankle and Tim's season with the Redmen came to an end.

Once the ankle had healed, Tim continued his rehabilitation by taking a job carrying bricks up a ladder in the construction of the Sudbury General Hospital. By the end of the summer, he was back in excellent physical condition.

Another summer, Tim had a job fighting forest fires in the woods near Cochrane. Well into his career, Tim usually opted for a summer job which involved manual labour, feeling the physical work could only help him when he was back on the ice in the fall.

But by no means did Tim enjoy all of these jobs. One he hated, and liked to remind himself of from time to time, was a two-week stint he did at Inco in the converter room,

Here's a letter sent by St. Mike's regarding Tim's athletic scholarship. There was some initial concern about his eyesight, which was always bad, and the fact that Tim was not a Catholic. But everything worked out in the end.

ST. MICHAEL'S COLLEGE

ST. MICHAEL'S COLLEGE
BAY AND ST. JOSEPH STS.
TORONTO 5

June 16, 1947

Dear Chas,

Excuse my delay in writing to you regarding Tim Horton, but it seems that since my return two months ago at the end of the season I have been doing nothing but mark papers some of which had accumulated for a month or more. I got the letters from Tim, and from Father Cano. I answered Tim only recently telling him that I could not give him a definite answer until later. You might tell him that as far as the scholarship goes, I can look after that, but Father Bondy demurred somewhat over the fact that he is not a catholic. He advised to get more information about him. I think it would help if you wrote a letter of recommendation to me, and if you got Father O'Leary to write one also. There is another non-Catholic on my list also, an established Junior player whom Joe P. would like to see here. Personally I think it does us no harm to have a couple as long as they are of good character and come well recommended. But I can not always get others to agree with me. I was impressed with Tim's letter. He seems to have ability. Did Bob Wilson change his mind about him because of the glasses? That was what we heard, that the pro scouts lost interest in him as a prospect because of his eyes. I would appreciate it if you talk to Tim, and not let him be discouraged by my letter, which was late and in which he might be disappointed. I still hope that I can get him in. *Hugh Mallon c.s.B.*
Best regards,

shoveling hot coals into a pit. Despite being covered head to foot with protective gear, hot cinders still found their way into his clothing, leaving small burn marks all over Tim's body. In later years, whenever hockey began to wear on him — whether it was injuries, or contract disputes — Tim would console himself with the fact that he was at least doing something he loved, and without it he could easily have ended up working in the mines.

In the end, Tim was scouted and signed by the Leafs. He received a sports scholarship to St. Michael's College in the fall of 1947. Tim had excelled in both hockey and football while at Sudbury High, with strength rather than size on his side. Tim's high-school teammate, the late Red McCarthy, several times expressed his belief that Tim could easily have ended up as "a great halfback" somewhere if he hadn't chosen to pursue a career in hockey.

While Tim was a regular churchgoer, as a Protestant, he had some reservations about attending a Catholic school. Tim requested and received a letter assuring him that he would not be required to attend religion classes. Only then did he accept the scholarship. Tim's teammates tended to sleep late Sunday morning after playing hockey the previous night, but Tim would be up attending services at the Metropolitan United Church. According to Father Bill O'Brien, one of Tim's teachers and now Archivist at

St. Mike's this habit was noted by the faculty, most of them Basilian fathers. Perhaps this is why Father Ted Flanagan was fond of telling me that Tim was one of the best Catholics he knew!

Tim played with St. Mike's for two years, and he was voted the team's most valuable player at the end of both seasons. When Tim was the star at St. Mike's again in his second year, people who watched him play began to peg him as a future NHLer. The Sudbury High team Tim had played on was a good one, and he had starred for a team called Holy Trinity in the Nickel District League, but Tim had played most of his minor hockey in Cochrane, a place which was a little out of the way even for hockey scouts. This low profile, when coupled with his exploits at St. Mike's, left people in hockey circles with the impression that he'd appeared out of nowhere.

THE HOCKEY PROGRAM at St. Mike's was famous for producing excellent hockey players who went on to star in the NHL. In addition to Tim, Red Kelly, Dick Duff, Dave Keon, Frank and Peter Mahovlich, and Ted Lindsay were all St. Mike's stars. The Wall of Fame in the Old Boy's Club at St. Mike's boasts dozens of pictures of successful hockey alumni, several of whom went on to star with the Maple Leafs.

On arrival in 1947, Tim was assigned rooms on the top floor of the college, in a section known as the "Jews Flat." Here there was room for only two or three students. The dorm was situated one floor down, and one floor below that was an area known as the "Irish Flat."

The St. Mike's Majors in Tim's first year. Tim's third from the left at the back with Gordie Hannigan and former Leaf great Joe Primeau (who would coach Tim later with the Maple Leafs) to Gord's left.
ST. MICHAEL'S COLLEGE YEARBOOK, 1948

11

As in high school, Tim was just a little better than an average student, but despite the time he devoted to prac‑ tising and playing hockey and football, he was always fairly serious about his studies. One of Tim's roommates in first year was Ted Carlton, who did not play hockey. He remem‑ bers Tim as a quiet, shy person, who despite his athletic skills was not overtly impressed with himself.

During his second year at St. Mike's, Tim roomed with another young Leaf prospect, Don Rope. Rope still vividly recalls his first day at the school, and his introduction to Tim Horton:

"I was signed by [Leaf scout] Squib Walker out of Winni‑ peg, and I reveled in the glory of being signed by the Toronto Maple Leafs, who were the number one team out in Western Canada. I came into Union Station and took a cab over to St. Mike's and wandered around wondering where I should go. I remember Father Crawley telling me, 'You're over there with Tim Horton.' At that time I didn't know who Tim was — we had a meeting out front and Father Crawley introduced me to him. But I still had no idea who he was until later that night when I got into bed and Tim started to do exercises. First he jumped up on the sill of the door (there was only about an inch there to grab) and he started doing chin-ups. I don't know how many he did, but if I said 50, that would be close. Then he started doing push-ups, and of course he was built like some Greek god. And I remember looking at him and thinking 'holy shit.'"

"The next day he took us down to Maple Leaf Gardens. Not just me, there were about a half a dozen of us from the hockey team. Tim took us through the back entrance of the

Gardens. He knew everybody, the guy at the door, and this guy and that guy — *everyone*. Of course for me to go to Maple Leaf Gardens, after listening to Foster Hewitt since 1934 . . . well the breath was just taken away from me. It was something I'd dreamt of as a kid . . . this was where I'd always dreamt of coming. I mean, I was awed. Then Timmy takes us into a room and there's Turk Broda — the first guy in my scrapbook as a little kid. Tim knew everybody and was so good with the guys."

"But it wasn't like he was showing off . . . you know, 'I know everybody.' He had a very quiet demeanor about him, reserved; he wasn't a showboat. Then we walked down Yonge Street where all the fruit vendors were, at least in those days, and Tim would be just the same — talking to these guys because he knew them. He knew so many people, it was like he'd been in Toronto for years. He'd only come to Toronto the year before, but at that time I don't think there was anybody he didn't know between St. Michael's College and Maple Leaf Gardens."

St. Mike's Majors, 1948. Left to right: Tim Horton, Bill McNamara, Ray Barry, Tom Shea, Joe Decourcy, Walter Clune, Gerry Fitzhenry. The Majors were not a successful team while Tim was there, but Tim was a standout, and was chosen best defenseman in the OHA in 1948–49 season.
ST. MICHAEL'S COLLEGE

TIM HAS BEEN A STAR ON THE MAJORS DEFENSE FOR TWO SEASONS.

TIM PLAYED MINOR HOCKEY IN COPPER CLIFF BEFORE COMING TO ST. MICHAEL'S

TIM HORTON

CHOSEN ~ THE BEST DEFENSEMAN IN THE JUNIOR "A" OHA DURING 1948-49

COPPER CLIFF

JOE HALLORAN. '49

TORONTO

St. Mike's yearbook illustration, 1949.

Don Rope had signed up for nine subjects that year while Tim was carrying only three. Rope remembers their study time was spent with Don working on a mountain of assignments while Tim, who could have been a serious distraction if he wanted to be, took to studying from the Bible. "Without becoming evangelistic," Rope recalls, "Tim began to quote from the Bible. It became a big factor in his life." Tim in fact, chose to take religion courses while he was at St. Mike's. His teacher, Father Flanagan, was a close friend of both Tim and myself until he died.

Joe Primeau's St. Mike's Squad Arrives Here For Spitfire Game

Toronto St. Michael's College Majors arrived in Windsor this afternoon confident of a win over Windsor Spitfires in the Ontario Hockey Association Junior "A" opener tonight at the Windsor Arena. The Dominion Memorial Cup champions of two seasons ago are touted as a much rejuvenated team this | year and are "all out" to regain the title for 1948-49. Fi members of the aggregation are shown above as they d trained at the C.N.R. station, left to right, Tom Shea, Go Hannigan, Coach Joe Primeau, Don Rope and Tom Horto The game will get under way at 8:30.

Because Don and Tim had been assigned the most spacious quarters in the Jew's Flat, the rest of the hockey team would gather there after dinner. More often than not an impromptu hockey game would break out, with the closets taking the place of goals. Mercifully, Father Crawley eventually moved a third roommate, who did not play hockey, to other quarters.

THE ST. MIKE'S MAJORS were not a successful team in either of the two years Tim played. Among the Majors' players in Tim's second year, only Tim and Gord Hannigan (who also played football) would eventually go on to play in the NHL (Hannigan would be a teammate of Tim's in both

Newspaper clipping from 1948, highlighting a game with the Windsor Spitfires. Don Rope is to Tim's right. Don became a teacher rather than pursuing a career in professional hockey, but he did play for the Canadian Olympic team.

15

Photo from a St. Mike's northern tour to Sudbury in 1949.

Pittsburgh and Toronto). Don Rope chose not to pursue a career in the NHL, but decided to continue his studies instead. He did, however, play on the Canadian Olympic team.

While at St. Mike's, in an effort to compensate for the team's lack of offense, Tim changed his playing style dramatically. Instead of hanging back on the blue line, Tim began carrying the puck more, rushing it up the ice in an effort to help out the offense. While some players felt Tim didn't pass enough (knowing Tim's suspect vision, others joked he simply couldn't see to pass), his point production increased dramatically. Sound defense, coupled with his new-found offensive flair, began to convince the Leafs they'd made a wise choice in signing him.

Years before the great Bobby Orr made the rushing defenseman an essential part of the game, 14,000 fans gathered at the Gardens on Sunday afternoons to cheer Tim's end-to-end rushes. Despite a superb year offensively and defensively from their star defenseman, the Majors finished next to last for the second straight year. Tim, however, was named the top defenseman in the OHA.

Horton's play may not have been enough to push St. Mike's into the playoffs, but it did a lot to catch the attention of the Maple Leafs' brass. During the fall of 1947,

Gordon Walker's "Hockey Gossip" column in the Leafs' program gave an account of a particularly fine game Tim played against the Galt Hornets, a game attended by Boston Bruins scout Harry (Hal) Cotton and Leaf owner Conn Smythe. Tim's end-to-end rush through the Galt team to score left the two Leaf executives shaking their heads, but it was the combination of skill and toughness which reportedly got the boss's attention, a hit on one of Galt's forwards which forced the opponent off on a stretcher:

In addition to hockey, Tim played rugby and did some running while he was at St. Mike's. Here he is at a track practice (third from left).
ST. MICHAEL'S COLLEGE

"At period's end, Smythe headed into the pressroom with that thoughtful look on his face. 'Just like Red Horner,' he murmured. 'He hits 'em just like Red. When Red was a junior he used to send them into the dressing room with their stomachs heaving, after getting a good belt at them. Horton's the same way. It almost made me sick to see the way Horvath went down after that check.'"

THIRTY-TWO NHL HOPEFULS, Tim among them, attended the Maple Leaf hockey school in St. Catharines in September, 1949. Players were there both to showcase and to improve their skills, and perhaps even stick around long enough to have a shot at playing an exhibition game with the pros a week later.

Tim with his friends back in Sudbury, 1950. Left to right: John Fingland, Tim's cousin Ron Owens, Tim (in his St. Mike's jacket), Bill Delaney, Ian Stewart, and Glen MacMillan (in the fedora).
GLEN MACMILLAN

Maple Leafs'
junior prospects,
before Tim's first
rookie camp,
St. Catharines,
1949. In addition
to Tim's St. Mike's
buddies, there's
also Andy Barbe,
who would be Tim's
teammate and
friend with the AHL
Pittsburgh Hornets.

ANDIDATES FOR SHEEPSKINS AT LEAFS' ST. CATHARINES ICE SCHOOL

J. FRICK Winnipeg   J. McKENZIE Brandon   D. ROPE St. Mike's   W. McCRACKEN Winnipeg   G. HUDSON Ottawa   T. BUCK St. Catharines

G. HANNIGAN St. Mike's   C. LUMSDEN Winnipeg   ANDY BARBE Coniston   F. SULLIVAN Toronto   T. HORTON Cochrane   A. CHILDS Fort William

Tim returned to St. Mike's in the fall to play with the Majors and continue his studies, as planned. Back in the 1940s, before the NHL draft came into existence, players were scouted, signed to a C-form, and developed for the big team in a manner far different than they are now. Teams were happy if they could set prospects up with teams close to home, where the big team could have a good look at them. George Armstrong played junior first in Stratford, then was asked to move to the Marlboros, who played out of Maple Leaf Gardens, so that the Leafs could monitor his progress. At the time they also wanted Tim to move over to the Marlboros, but when he didn't want to leave St. Mike's they left him alone for another year.

"I was playing in Stratford," Armstrong remembers, "which at that time was about a five-hour car ride [to Toronto]. When I refused to go to the Marlboros at first, they suspended me. So I had to go. But they let Tim stay at St. Mike's for another year."

After Tim's second year starring at St. Mikes, Leafs owner Conn Smythe, anxious to bring the Marlies up to the level of Memorial Cup contenders, decided again that he wanted Tim to move from St. Mike's over to the Marlies. Again, Tim balked.

As a student on an athletic scholarship, Tim's classes were covered and room and board were provided. In addition, for playing hockey he received the princely sum of ten dollars weekly. By comparison, a Junior A player of Tim's caliber was typically paid $50 a week. Armstrong, like Horton, had his room and board paid for, but also received $175 a week. Still, Tim was getting a good education at St. Mike's. His ready wit, engaging nature, and laid-back personality made him one of the most popular students at the school, quite apart from his star status as an athlete. As a player he was thriving under the discipline of the college and his coach, former Leaf great Joe Primeau. But more than anything, Tim hated the idea of playing against his old teammates. "Tim told them, 'If I'm going to play junior, I'm gonna play junior for St. Mike's!' and that's all there was to it," Armstrong recalls.

Still, Tim was well aware that the road led from St. Mike's to the NHL. Dick Duff, Tim's future teammate and star Maple Leaf left-winger, played at St. Mike's a few years after Tim, and recalls that there were only two ways to get to the

Great Leaf goalie Turk Broda flanked by Tim and Gordie Hannigan, at the 1949 rookie camp. "Tim [once] took me and a half dozen of us from the [St. Mike's] hockey team down to Maple Leaf Gardens. . . . Timmy takes us through the back entrance and into a room, and there's Turk Broda — the first guy in my scrapbook when I was a little kid. . . . I mean, I was awed. . . ." (— Don Rope)

IMPERIAL OIL LIMITED, TUROFSKY COLLECTION, HOCKEY HALL OF FAME

Gordie Hannigan and Tim getting some advice from Joe Primeau during one of the Leafs' rookie camps. Gord was always a very good friend of Tim's. He died very young — at age 37, of a heart attack.

IMPERIAL OIL LIMITED, TUROFSKY COLLECTION, HOCKEY HALL OF FAME

Leafs in those days — through the St. Mike's system or through the Marlies:

"Young players in those days would always get caught up with the idea of the people who had preceded them. Timmy probably knew at that time that Gus Mortson and Jimmy Thomson and Ted Lindsay had been at St. Mike's ahead of him. Tod Sloan and Red Kelly as well. For me, a few years later, it was guys like Timmy who we looked up to. A young guy at that age would see these guys with the Leafs and see a direction he was supposed to follow, and he knew the pros were watching him and expecting him to follow in their footsteps." In the end, Tim was given a second option — he could move to the Marlies or turn pro and play for the Pittsburgh Hornets of the American Hockey League.

"When we first signed what they called the 'C-form' with the Maple Leafs — we got $100 with that — the contract said we were the property of the Toronto Maple Leafs, and when they offered us a contract as professional hockey player we had to sign it," says Armstrong. "We *had* to sign it. If we refused to sign that contract, they could suspend us." Armstrong was put under the same pressure by the Leafs the previous year before reaching a compromise which had him playing for the Marlies, and Armstrong thinks the similar pressure tactics were used on Tim. Unable to decide, Tim called his parents in North Bay

Tim and his father in North Bay, around 1950. I always thought
Tim took after his mother, and Tim's brother Gerry looked
very much like Oak; but they sure look alike in this picture.

for their opinion. While Oak would have preferred that Tim stay at St. Mike's and finish his education, he wisely left the decision to his son.

A week after training camp opened, Tim signed a contract to join the Pittsburgh Hornets. He would be paid $3,000 a year, with a $3500 signing bonus. Even in 1948, $3,000 was not a lot of money — but it was a little more than most people might make in a year, and Tim was glad to have it. As soon as his cheque cleared, Tim went out and bought himself his first car, a 1949 Mercury.

During a benefit game with the Maple Leafs before the 1949 season, Tim received his first full write-up in a major Toronto newspaper. *Globe and Mail* reporter Jim Vipond immediately pegged Tim (who set up both Pittsburgh goals in a 4–2 loss to the Leafs) as NHL material. Vipond praised

Illustration for the *Post-Gazette* in Pittsburgh, just after Tim turned pro in the fall of '49.
AUTHORS' COLLECTION

CAPS

FLYERS

THE COMING WEEK MAY DECIDE THE HORNETS' PLAYOFF CHANCES ·· THEY PLAY ST. LOUIS ON WEDNESDAY AND INDIANAPOLIS NEXT SATURDAY AND SUNDAY!

BACK LINE BATTLER!

THE AGGRESSIVE HORTON IS RATED AS A GREAT PROSPECT BY THE MAPLE LEAFS·· HE'S FROM ST. MIKE'S COLLEGE, TORONTO.

ROUGH AND READY ROOKIE DEFENSEMAN··

Tim HORTON.

BURNLEY

Tim, as he looked during his second year with the Hornets. The Leafs were a great team at this point (they won the Stanley Cup in 1949–50), otherwise I think Tim would have broken into the NHL sooner. When you consider that only about 120 players were in the NHL during the six-team league, the level of play in the American League was extremely good in those days.

the second assist as "particularly spectacular, as he skated through the entire Leaf team to put the puck on the stick of a waiting Andy Barbe." Vipond was also struck by Horton's defensive skills and toughness: "Defensively, Horton . . . slipped into the Leafs with absolutely no regard for reputations. He thrilled a sellout crowd with a bumping duel with Bill Ezinicki in the second period and was in the thick of the action at all times."

At the Hornet's training camp, Tim's lingering problems with his eyesight finally prompted someone to set up an appointment with team optometrist Dr. Tom Pashby, the same Dr. Pashby who has done so much to promote safety in sports in Canada, raising funds through dinners, golf tournaments and the like to fund the research and development of safety equipment for minor sports — helmets, mouth guards, neck protectors, etc. Tim was diagnosed as short-sighted with severe astigmatism in one eye (his vision in his left eye was 40/400), problems which could not be easily solved with glasses alone. Dr. Pashby escorted Tim to Brent Laboratories in Toronto, where a dental dam was used to make molds of the entire eye. The molds were then used to fashion a hard contact — which covered the entire eyeball — which Tim could wear during a game.

Wearing these strange ancestors of contact lenses was no picnic. The lenses were prone to fogging, and had to be removed and replaced between periods when he started seeing rainbows. They did, however, significantly improve Tim's vision and he put up with them as best he could. Despite their awkwardness, Tim wore the contacts consistently until his big injury with the Maple Leafs in 1955. Unfortunately, two of our daughters inherited Tim's eyesight — and Jeri has finally had success using contacts.

Not too long afterwards Tim also took to wearing glasses off the ice — big clumsy black-framed things with one lens so thick that it made the shape of his eye seem distorted. I've got more than one photo of Tim at a party mugging it for the camera in those goofy glasses. But Tim didn't seem to care — for the first time in his life, he could actually see properly.

The home rink in Pittsburgh for the Hornets was Duquesne Gardens, a converted streetcar barn directly across the street from St. Paul Cathedral, and not too far from Forbes

Pittsburgh Hornets Hockey Team
SEASON 1950-51

Field which, until Three Rivers Stadium was built, housed the Steelers football team and the baseball Pirates. Nearby was the University of Pittsburgh, Carnegie Museum, some leading hospitals — the educational and cultural centre of the city. Most of the players made their homes in the East Liberty district, in older homes converted to apartments. In his first two seasons with the Hornets, Tim roomed with Ray Hannigan (brother of Gord), Andy Barbe, and John McClelland (a future coach with the Leafs).

At that time, Tim was known among his teammates for his frugality. When I first met Tim, his nickname was "Thrifty." Andy Barbe found Tim to be extremely shy, naturally, but on the rare occasions Tim drank in those days, a few beers tended to loosen him up. With his inhibitions removed, however, he showed the "mischievous" streak (as George Armstrong would later describe it) that his teammates would both enjoy and dread for the rest of Tim's career.

Popular with all of the players, Tim formed a close friendship with Frank Mathers, one of the Hornet defensemen.

The 1950–51 Pittsburgh Hornets. Tim's standing behind coach Bob Davidson in the middle. George Armstrong is number 8 (two over on Tim's left), Andy Barbe (16) is on the far right in the front row. The goalies were Al Rollins and "Gil" Mayer, both of whom played briefly for the Leafs.

Tim on a rush during his second season with Pittsburgh. With both St. Mike's and the Hornets, Tim was always a rushing defense- man, but when he came up with Toronto, he was forced to work within the Leafs' defensive system.

HOCKEY HALL OF FAME

In a game against Buffalo one year, after a particularly vicious hit on Mathers, Tim chased the offending party (Harry Dick, who weighed close to 220 pounds) around the ice, put him in a bear hug, picked him up, and threw him over the boards. At the time, Tim weighed no more than 165. Though he was never a big man, Tim's prodigious strength was never in doubt among teammates and foes alike.

E ARLY IN TIM'S SECOND season in Pittsburgh, before I'd met him, I attended my first hockey game. At that time I knew nothing about the game. Still, Tim immediately stood out. He was a strong skater, *that* I could see, but I admit that once I'd noticed him, the game itself became secondary to watching him. Tim was the first star of the game on this night, so he must have played well. After the game I cut Tim's picture out of the program and put it up on my mirror at home. It was up there on my mirror for a year before I actually met him.

Several years earlier, my father and I had signed a contract with the Ice Capades which allowed me special privileges in Duquesne Gardens. I was able to use the Gardens ice for skating lessons and practice on Saturday afternoons and Sunday mornings, and to skate at all the public sessions free of charge. I had a full-time job, but all my evenings — with the exceptions of Wednesday and Saturday nights — were spent skating at Duquesne Gardens. John Harris owned both the Hornets and the Ice Capades in Pittsburgh, and had a clause in all employees' contracts forbidding fraternization between the two groups, although Harris himself was married to one of the stars of the Ice Capades, Donna Atwood.

The clause had never proved to be a problem for me. I had spoken to a few of the players from time to time, and had even been invited out on a date by one of them, but I was at the Gardens to skate, and in any case, I was already dating a nice young man I had been seeing since high school.

One man who spent a lot of time at the arena and seemed to be a friend of some of the players was Adolph Donadeo. Adolph approached me one night while I was waiting for some very young hockey players to leave the ice. He had Tim in tow, and after some small talk asked me if I'd ever

Tim's twenty-first birthday party. That's Adolph Donadeo in the sweater and bow-tie, the man who introduced me to Tim, his sister Rose, and teammates Ray Hannigan (Gordie's brother), and George Costello to her right. The man to Tim's left is Rose's husband.
AUTHORS' COLLECTION

met Tim Horton. We were introduced, and spoke for a few minutes while the players left the ice. Then I went for my evening skate as usual. After my skate, while I was having a hot chocolate, Tim reappeared.

"Can I take you home?" he asked. "Or don't you take rides home from strangers?"

At this point I felt I knew him — I had been looking at his picture since that first game — so I said fine. It was a long drive from the Gardens in Oakland to my home in Mt. Oliver. Despite Tim's shyness (which I found very appealing) we found lots to talk about, and we spent hours chatting, parked out in front of my house. I was 18 at the time; I had a curfew, and my father was very strict, but he was working nights and my mother was a very sound sleeper so Tim would drop me off minutes before my Dad arrived

Promotional item for the Pittsburgh *Post-Gazette*, 1951.
AUTHORS' COLLECTION

GET THE NUMBER OF THAT TRUCK!

TOUGH TIM REALLY CHECKS 'EM!

HE CELEBRATED HIS 21ST BIRTHDAY LAST WEEK.

THE LEAGUE-LEADING CLEVELAND BARONS COLLIDE WITH THE WASPS IN TONIGHT'S IMPORTANT CLASH AT THE GARDENS!

BURNLEY 6

Tim HORTON
GREAT YOUNG DEFENSEMAN OF THE HORNETS.. ONE OF THE REASONS WHY ENEMY TEAMS HARDLY EVER GET MORE SHOTS ON GOAL THAN THE WASPS.

Tim with his brother Gerry, around 1950. Gerry was also a good hockey player, getting as far as Junior A with the Oshawa Generals. Gerry literally died with his skates on in 1994, while playing hockey up in North Bay.
AUTHORS' COLLECTION

home. Tim began calling regularly. I started attending all the Hornets' home games, and the two of us completely ignored the rule against fraternizing. King Clancy, then the Hornets' coach, was aware we were seeing each other, but after talking to Tim, he chose to ignore it.

The Hornets were a good team that year, making the AHL finals before bowing out to the Cleveland Barons (who were backstopped by Tim's future Toronto teammate, Johnny Bower).

A FEW DAYS AFTER the season ended, Tim returned home, this time to North Bay, where his parents had moved in 1949.

Through successive summers Tim had worked on a tobacco farm (a job which even Tim found to be too much for him), picking weeds in the Holland Marsh, and delivering beer for Brewer's Retail in North Bay.

Correspondence became quite regular that summer between North Bay and Pittsburgh, and Tim returned for a visit in July with his brother Gerry and Merv Delaney, a friend from North Bay. I had arranged for my vacation to coincide with Tim's visit, and I set up dates for Gerry and Merv with a few of my girlfriends. It was a great time for everyone, and by the end of the two weeks Tim announced to me one night that I was the girl he intended to marry.

The proposal came after a few beers, however, and I decided not to take it too seriously at the time.

This was the summer of 1951, the same summer Leaf hero Bill Barilko's plane disappeared while on a fishing trip in late August. What truly happened to him will never be known, but more than a decade later, the wreckage

Milt Dunnell's *Star* column about Tim, the year before he made the Maple Leafs, quoting Eddie Shore, who always thought the world of Tim. I once spent an entire train ride talking with Eddie Shore without for a minute knowing who Eddie was.

TORONTO STAR

18 TORONTO DAILY STAR: Sat., April 7, 1951

Speaking on Sport
By MILT DUNNELL — Sports Editor

Nomination For Next Year's Rookie

HAP DAY (three successive Stanley Cups, remember?) chuckled when he saw Eddie Shore, the one-time Mr. Hockey, wander into the Gardens. Shore may have been lured by the Boston Bruins, who were working out for tonight's joust with the Leafs. During his years in big league hockey, Shore is supposed to have dug more gold from the Boston coffers than the sourdoughs took from the Klondyke. Whatever he got, he was worth, as they've found out since. There's nothing wrong with hockey in beantown that another Shore wouldn't cure.

"The night Pittsburgh Hornets scored six goals on Eddie's team in Springfield," Day laughed, "Shore got out on the ice and was looking around the back of the net. Some leather-lunged fan yelled out: 'No sense looking there, Shore. Those goals went in from the front.'"

Shore, it developed, had important news. He was able to name the winner of next season's rookie award in the National Hockey league. And he wasn't thinking about either Glen Skov of the Detroits or Boom-Boom Geoffrion of Canadiens, who already are strong candidates for the 1952 Calder cup.

The winner, said Shore, without qualification, will be Tim Horton, who happens to belong to the Leafs. If Shore is right, Horton would be the first defence man ever to cop the award. Leafs hoped to do it this year with Hugh Bolton, but the big rearguard spent most of the season on the limp. He was shipped down to Pittsburgh when he was ready to resume work.

"Horton can skate rings around any defence player in the league," Shore proclaimed. He didn't mean the American league. He referred to the N.H.L. "He's the best-looking super-star I've seen in 10 years. He carries the puck; he stick-handles. There's nothing he can't do. And talk about color . . . if the officials will just stop some of the hooking and holding, he will thrill more people in five minutes next winter than most players will thrill in three games."

Shore hazarded a prediction that, with Fern Flaman and Horton wearing Gardens spangles, Leafs would have no worries about the right side of their defence for quite a few years.

Pittsburgh Hornets Hockey Team
SEASON 1951-1952

of his plane was found in the bush some 50 miles north of Cochrane. The Leafs had won four Stanley Cups in five years, with Barilko scoring the famous overtime goal which clinched the Cup that spring.

In the fall, Frank Sullivan, Frank Mathers, and Tim were invited to try out at the Leafs' training camp. As early as April, Eddie Shore, the legendary Bruins defenseman and scout, had picked Horton not only to make the big team, but to contend for the Calder Trophy as rookie-of-the-year. In the *Toronto Star*'s April 7th edition, sports editor Milt Dunnell quoted Shore singing Tim's praises: " 'Horton can skate rings around any defense player in the [NHL],' Shore proclaimed. . . . 'He's the best-looking super-star I've seen in 10 years. He carries the puck, he stick-handles. There's nothing he can't do. And talk about colour . . . he will thrill more people in five minutes next winter than most players will thrill in three games.' "

Eddie Shore was always a big Horton booster. There's a funny story about the day I met Eddie, which was the next

The Hornets' Calder Championship team, Tim's last year in Pittsburgh. Tim is on the far left in the first row; Frank Mathers (#2), Tim's defense partner and the best man at our wedding, is second on Tim's right; and coach King Clancy is next to Frank.

31

year during the playoffs. The Hornets were playing the Hershey Bears and I didn't know Eddie Shore from anybody. I took a train from Pittsburgh to Harrisburg, Pennsylvania, and then you had to take a bus to Hershey. A man sat down next to me on the train and asked If I was going down for the hockey game, he was too, and so on. We discussed how I was getting married to one of the players at the end of the season; he asked "to whom?" and I told him "Horton." And then he proceeded to tell me all about him — he always thought the world of Tim — but even after all of this I still didn't know who he was. We talked all the way to Hershey, got off the bus and walked into the lobby together where Tim was standing waiting for me. Tim's eyes lit up — I mean, there I am walking in with Eddie Shore. And Tim says, "How in the world did you ever meet Eddie Shore?" It took Tim telling me before I knew who he was.

T HE LEAFS WERE STILL a powerhouse in those days, which probably helps explain why Tim was in Pittsburgh as long as he was. But now they were looking for someone who played like Barilko. Tim was certainly tough enough, but his end-to-end rushing was not a good fit with coach Hap Day's defensive style, and in any case the Leafs felt Tim's work in his own end could still be improved.

Some action in front of the Hornets' net during the 1951–52 season. The goalie should be Gil Mayer, but it's hard to tell who the others are. Tim (#3) was named assistant captain that year.

Leading Hornets Still Face Stiff Challenge From Cleveland Barons

TIM HORTON   **DORIS MICHALEK**
Mt. Oliver miss to wed Hornet star at season's end.

*   *   *

Wasps Hold Eight-Point Spread But Each Team Has 16 Games Left in Season

By JIMMY JORDAN
Post-Gazette Sports Writer

The American Hockey League season headed into the stretch today, with the title-hungry Hornets still facing a continuous challenge from the Cleveland Barons who have been trying desperately to overtake the high-flying Pittsburghers in recent weeks.

The Wasps hold an eight-point (four games) lead over the Barons, and each has 16 more games to play, including two between the rivals, one at The Gardens and one at Cleveland.

But that eight-point spread looked anything but comfortable as the two clubs prepared for the stretch run. The Hornets shut out Indianapolis at The Gardens Saturday night, while Cleveland was beating Syracuse, 5-2 to keep on the tail of the Craig Street icers.

The Hornets had an open date yesterday, but Coach King Clancy decided it would not be a complete day of rest. He ordered them on the ice for a fast one-hour workout to get them ready for Wednesday's invasion of the St. Louis Flyers.

Due to tonight's basketball game between Duquesne and St. Bonaventure, and a wrestling show Tuesday night, there will be no opportunity for practice again before Wednesday unless Clancy takes the club to Johnstown, as he did two weeks ago.

Saturday night's game was a rough, close-checking affair. After a scoreless first period, Jim Morrison scored the first goal for Pittsburgh after 18 seconds of play in the second period. Larry Zeidel was in the penalty box at the time, and Morrison broke away at the blue line for the tally, with Johny McLellan and Pete Backor getting assists.

Japs Sweep Titles

BOMBAY, Feb. 10 (AP)—Japan's Hiroji Satoh became the world table tennis singles champion today, completing virtual Japanese domination of the championships here. Satoh whipped Hungary's Josef Kozcian, 21-19, 21-17, 21-14, after the Japs had swept the men's and women's doubles titles.

Article from the Pittsburgh *Post-Gazette* announcing our engagement. We originally planned the wedding for the 17th of April, but over dinner one night Hornets' owner John Harris quietly suggested that we choose another date. There was a game scheduled for that night.

In fact, early in Tim's stay with the Hornets, Conn Smythe had been pushing Hornets' coach Bob Davidson to move Tim from defense to right wing to take advantage of his skating and his shot. "I always felt Horton belonged on the wing," Smythe was quoted saying in a 1956 Toronto *Star* article. "When I signed him it was with the intention of converting him into a right-winger." Davidson had apparently tried, but Tim had stubbornly refused the switch. Tim quickly became the best rushing defenseman in the league, and the idea was dropped. Many years later with the Leafs, Tim would in fact play some right wing for several games (in addition to his regular shift on defense). He did quite well, in fact, though I think he would have loved to try his luck at centre.

In the end, Hugh Bolton — who had spent part of the previous season with the Leafs — was chosen to fill Barilko's spot.

Tim scored the tying goal and Ray Hannigan, the winner, in the Calder Cup-clinching game in Hershey. The next morning a huge crowd met the team train in Pittsburgh. It was the city's first championship hockey team.

Champion Hornets Get Big Welcome Home

This is a section of the huge crowd which greeted the Hornets as they returned yesterday afternoon from their victory in Providence.

A BRASS band and a crowd of several hundred hockey fans greeted the Hornets at Pennsylvania Station as they arrived in Pittsburgh yester- | day after winning the first Calder Cup in the club's 16 seasons in the American Hockey League. It took them a long time to get there but Ray Hannigan's | goal in the second overtime period of the sixth game of the championship series at Providence Sunday night decided it, 3-2.

When Tim returned to the Hornets from rookie camp this time, there was some disappointment. He arranged to meet me at the arena when the Hornets came back to town. I was there skating when he arrived, but Tim stayed only a few minutes and left without even saying hello. We had been writing all summer and so his behaviour seemed strange to me. But two days later he called and he was his old self again. We saw each other that evening and were together every available moment for the rest of the season. Hornet coach King Clancy obviously wouldn't have been thrilled at the prospect of losing his star defenseman, so I don't think he was unhappy when Bolton got the Toronto job ahead of Tim.

In the end, it was Clancy (who always was a personal favorite of both Tim and myself) who helped Tim develop to the next level. Tim did get to put on the Maple Leaf jersey after all that winter — for four games — replacing injured Leaf rearguard Bill Juzda. In its write-up of the first of those games, against the Chicago Blackhawks, the Toronto *Star* praised Tim for his improved play since rookie camp: Tim "rushed right up the ice from the opening face-off," appeared "calm at all times," and "carried the puck out of his own end well."

Back with Pittsburgh, Tim and his teammates held off a late-season surge by the Cleveland Barons to win the Western Division title of the AHL for the first time in team

34

history. Paced by terrific rookies Frank Sullivan, Gord Hannigan, and Bob Hassard, a solid defense led by Tim and Frank Mathers, the scoring of Ray Hannigan and Andy Barbe, and spectacular goaltending from Gil Mayer, the Hornets advanced through the playoffs and won the AHL's Calder Cup with a 4–2 series win over the Providence Reds. In the championship-clinching game, Ray Hannigan potted the cup-winner in double overtime to give the Hornets their first AHL championship. Tim had scored an unassisted goal to tie the game in the second period, but his best work was probably done in front of his own net, helping the team weather several power plays, including one stretch of close to three minutes in the first period when the Hornets were down two men.

When the team arrived back in town at about five in the afternoon the next day, several hundred fans (and a brass band) met the train at Pennsylvania Station. Pittsburgh wasn't a big hockey town — Duquesne Arena only held about 3,000 people — but it was the first Calder Cup for

LOOKING FOR ANOTHER—Coach King Clancy (right) and Owner John Harris of the Hornets shown with the Teddy Okes trophy, presented to the Wasps last night for winning the western division title of the American Hockey League. It was the first time the Hornets have won the cup since they entered the league in 1936. Now they hope to win the Calder Cup in the playoff series.

Clancy and team owner John Harris. Harris dated one of the stars of the ice capades, who practised in Duquesne Gardens, as did the Hornets.

35

the Hornets and the first hockey championship in Pittsburgh since Lionel Conacher's Yellow Jackets won the United States Hockey Association championship back in the mid-1920s.

It's worth remembering that the NHL was still just a six-team league at this time and the best of the AHL teams were excellent by today's standards. Years later, when sizing up the talent on that 1951–52 Calder Cup team, King Clancy would tell me he felt that particular Hornets team was good enough to play competitively against the Stanley Cup winners of recent years.

T WO DAYS LATER, Tim and I were married, with Tim's defense partner Frank Mathers as the best man. The wedding was a story in itself. We'd set the date for April 17th,

Our marriage licence. Tim and I had already delayed the wedding a week, and if the Hornets hadn't clinched in Hershey, we would probably have gotten married, then taken the guests down to watch Tim play game six of the AHL championship, which would have been scheduled for the 23rd.

OFFICE OF THE REGISTER OF WILLS

County of Allegheny

CITY-COUNTY BLDG.
414 GRANT STREET • PITTSBURGH, PA 15219-2471
(412) 355-4180

JAY COSTA, JR.
REGISTER OF WILLS
AND
CLERK OF ORPHANS' COURT

TO WHOM IT MAY CONCERN:

I hereby certify that the following and attached documents represent a true and correct copy of the original MARRIAGE RECORD filed in this office:

I, *A Gordon MacLennan*, hereby certify that on the *23rd* day of *April* one thousand nine hundred and *52* at *Pittsburgh* *Miles G. Horton* and *Delores Michalek* were, by me *Married* ( ) united in marriage, in accordance with license issued by the Clerk of the Orphans' Court of Allegheny County, Pennsylvania,

Numbered *6352* Series **TWO** SIGN HERE *A Gordon MacLennan*
Minister of the Gospel, Justice of the Peace, or Alderman

Address of person officiating *5701 Centre Ave* *Pgh. 32, Pa.*

IMPORTANT NOTICE

Dated: *2-16-93*

JAY COSTA, JR.
CLERK OF ORPHANS' COURT
DIVISION, COURT OF COMMON
PLEAS OF ALLEGHENY COUNTY,
PENNSYLVANIA

(MLB #7 9/92)

because Tim wanted to be married when the season was finished and because he had a job offer in North Bay and he wanted to get back. One night John Harris took us out for dinner and when we told him about our plans, he suggested we might change the date — there was a game scheduled that night. So we postponed the wedding until Wednesday the 23rd, but as it turned out there was the possibility of a playoff game that night as well. Thankfully, Sunday night proved to be the last game of the year. Before that we'd been talking about how we might have to take all the wedding guests down to the hockey game. We didn't know what we were going to do. If the Hornets hadn't won the championship on Sunday, Tim would have played a hockey game on our wedding night.

A lot of the Hornet players weren't at the wedding. It was a small wedding and I'm not sure they were all invited. In any case, most teammates were from Canada and would have left immediately after the season ended. King Clancy was there, and John Harris and his wife. Andy Barbe, Tim's roommate, also attended and his wife-to-be Frances

Wedding day I woke up with a strep throat, I had a fever of about 105, and I had to go to a doctor and get my throat swabbed to get through the wedding. That's Frank Mathers on my right, my girlfriend Helen Ference, my brother Bernie and sister Alice on Tim's right, and my niece Susie in front.

Swearinger sang at the wedding and was fabulous — she was a performer with the Pittsburgh Opera Company. Tim and I had spent a lot of time with them that winter and had become very close friends. Tim's brother, Gerry, came down from North Bay for the wedding to represent the family as Tim's parents were unable to attend.

Like most weddings, this one had a few glitches. I woke up with strep throat and a fever of 105 and had to get my throat swabbed to get through the day. It rained all day, and all the way down to Florida. We had a two-week honeymoon, drove back, and then went directly from Pittsburgh to North Bay.

I had never been to Canada and didn't know what to expect. I knew Gerry pretty well, but I'd never met Tim's parents; we'd tried to hitch up a couple of times when Tim was playing a game in Buffalo but the weather had never cooperated.

It was the first time I'd ever been that far north. We bought a cottage on Trout Lake, near North Bay. It was a small, very private cottage on an acre of land with outdoor plumbing; the nearest neighbour was a mile and a half away. Because it was common for people to report sightings of bears in the area, when Tim was away at work I'd stay in the house with all the doors locked. When I needed to use the outdoor facilities at night, I insisted that Tim escort me with a shotgun, much to the amusement of summer visitors. And we had a lot of visitors that summer. "Army" was there to help paint the interior, Gord Hannigan came down with a few friends, and most of my family and a few girlfriends came up from Pittsburgh. Tim's cousin Millie from Cochrane came to stay with me a lot, thank God. It took a long time for me to get acclimatized to the "great outdoors."

TIM ATTENDED HIS THIRD Leaf rookie camp in St. Catharines in the fall. Tim and Frank Mathers had been named American League All-Stars earlier that year after the playoffs were over. Gus Mortson was traded to Chicago in

Friends of Tim's knew someone who ran a bakery down in Pittsburgh, and they made a gift of this splendid wedding cake.

This is on our honeymoon in Daytona Beach and Tim washing his '52 Mercury. He'd had a 1949 Mercury, but driving home from Sudbury the summer before, Tim was diddling with the radio dial and drove it into a pile of rocks.

early September (along with Ray Hannigan) as part of the deal which brought goalie Harry Lumley to the Leafs. Bill Judza retired after the 1951–52 season. As far as the Toronto papers were concerned, that left only Fern Flaman and Jim Thomson as Leafs assured of blue line jobs, which meant Tim was in a training camp battle with fellow newcomers Leo Boivin, Hugh Bolton, and Frank Sullivan.

Joe Primeau, Tim's coach from St. Mike's, had moved on to become head coach of the Maple Leafs, and both King Clancy and Conn Smythe had been high on Tim all along. Still, Tim's letters home from St. Catharines indicated that Tim felt that he was destined for another year in Pittsburgh: "I felt good today in practice, but things, in my opinion and a few others, have already been settled," Tim wrote. "They know who their team is now. Does it ever make me mad when I think of it, so I will just stop."

Of course, Tim did make the Leafs out of training camp, but it took him years to feel settled with the team. He was always expecting to be dropped. Primeau and he were friends, but Leaf GM Hap Day kept him on tenterhooks the

This would be just after our honey-moon, driving up to North Bay. I didn't meet Tim's parents until after the wedding. We'd tried to hitch up a few times when Tim was on the road with the Hornets, but the weather had never co-operated.
At right is the same summer; Tim at Trout Lake, north of Sudbury. It was a mile and a half to the nearest cottage, and when Tim went into town to work I used to sit inside with the doors all locked. I'd never been that far north before and I was terrified of bears.

whole time. Hap insisted that the team put defense first, and for years Tim would insist that he was never really able to play his game with the Leafs. Tim never played another minor league game, but it took nearly six years, until Punch Imlach was hired as General Manager in 1958, before Tim really felt he had made the team. Tim went on to play the next 23 years in the NHL, 19 with the Leafs. He would play more games (1,185) with the Leafs than any player except George Armstrong (who played two more). To date, only

Welland HOUSE
ST. CATHARINES ONTARIO, CANADA
PHONE MU 5-7371

Monday nite.

Dear Lori.

How are you, I am fine. Just got in from a show that was the worst in History and am ready for bed. Got your letter to-day & was glad to hear from you. Also had one from home and Mom seems lonely as Pop was away all week when we left. Other than that there isn't a lot more that's new. I felt good to-day in practice but things, in my opinion and a few others, have already been settled and they know who their team is now. Does it ever make me mad when I think of it so I will just stop. Had two practices to-day so didn't go golfing or anything. There just isn't anything to do or write about these days. All the radio is full of these days is the fighting between the political boys in the states and what big crooks they are. And you always stick

Welland HOUSE
ST. CATHARINES ONTARIO, CANADA
PHONE MU 5-7371

2.

up for them. Well little wife I love you very much and I'll say so long for now and get some sleep. It was pretty cool here when we got out of the show so I guess winter is on it's way again. Say Hello for me to all.

I love you very much

Jim X XXX.

P.S. Here it is Tues. morning after breakfast and I have to get an envelope so thought I'd say good-morning. There is a nice song on the radio Slim Whitman and his 'Indian love call' it's pretty nice. Give Jr. a little tap for me eh.

I love you.

XXXX.

Gordie Howe played more seasons in the NHL than Tim Horton, and Tim stands fourth on the all-time list in NHL games played behind Gordie Howe, Alex Delvecchio, and Johnny Bucyk. He would score 458 points in Toronto, 12th on the Leafs all-time scoring list (one behind Lanny McDonald), and despite playing in a defense-oriented era, Tim still sits second in scoring all-time among Leafs defensemen, after Borje Salming.

The Leafs opened the 1952–53 season at home, on October 11th, with a 6–2 loss to the Chicago Blackhawks. It was Tim's sixth NHL game, but his first as a Leaf regular. Twenty-three years later, Tim would also play his last NHL game at Maple Leaf Gardens, a 4–2 loss to the Leafs as a member of the Buffalo Sabres. Tim had injured his face in practice a few days earlier (a broken cheekbone, Tim suspected); still, he completed two periods that night before the pain became too severe to play. Despite sitting out the third, he was named one of the game's three stars. Roughly six hours after he left the Gardens' ice that night, Tim would be gone.

This is a letter from training camp, the year Tim made the big club. "I felt good today in practice," he writes, "but things, in my opinion and a few others, have already been settled and they know who their team is now. Does it ever make me mad when I think of it, so I will just stop." He never played in the minors again, but it took Tim years to feel secure with the Leafs.

Tim in his rookie year with Joe Primeau. Tim loved King Clancy, and played his best hockey under Punch Imlach, but Primeau was always Tim's favorite as far as coaches were concerned.

11

'The Pony Express'

Tim was the only player who could really carry the puck
for Toronto. . . . If they needed the puck out of their
end, he was the guy. He was skating fast . . . and he must
have had his head down and Gadsby caught him just
right, because you could hear the snap all over the rink.
I was up in the greens and I heard it very clearly.
— *Frank Mahovlich*

O NCE WE KNEW Tim would be playing with the Leafs that
first season, we bought a house at 1382 Warden Avenue
(near Ellesmere) in Scarborough. It was a new house in a new
subdivision; we bought it sight unseen from a plan. Unfortunately, the plan didn't have a railroad marked on it — that
surprise awaited us when we moved in. For years we put up
with trains passing nearby at all hours of the day and night
— it must have been the main line to somewhere.

Though Tim was still far from relaxed about his position
with the Leafs, he continued to gain ground and attention
as an NHL regular. Early in his first season, a groin injury to
Leafs' stalwart Fern Flaman prompted coach Primeau to go
with a rookie tandem of Tim and Leo Boivin on defense.
Though the two had never played together as teammates
in Pittsburgh, they gelled right away, with Boivin's solid
defense a good match for Tim's rushing ability in a 2–2 tie
against the Hawks. In a Red Burnett article in the *Star*,
long-time Blackhawks broadcaster Joe Farrell was particularly impressed with Tim, comparing him to Leaf great
King Clancy and giving him "a chance to become one of

43

Tim with teammate
Ray Timgren, who
lived across the street
and two blocks down
from our first house
in Scarborough.

the league's greats" if he continued to develop. In the end,
the Leafs needed help most on the left side, and converted
Tim, despite some initial problems, to left defense, where
he played with veteran Jim Thomson.

Tim with King Clancy,
before King's debut as
Leafs coach in 1953. King
was always a favorite of
both Tim and myself, and
Tim was honoured when
Clancy asked him to wear
#7, King's number during
his great career with the
Maple Leafs.

Turofsky

"Begorra, be gettin' some goals," coach King Clancy passes instruction across the boards
to Tim Horton, the defenseman who will be wearing King's old No. 7 in Clancy's debut at
Maple Leaf Gardens tonight. Chicago Black Hawks oppose Leafs in the NHL opener.

The Leafs started strongly in the 1952–53 season, a tough team which led the league in penalty minutes and was bolstered in part by an unusually strong crop of rookies which included Tim, Leo Boivin, George Armstrong, Gord Hannigan, Ron Stewart, and Jim Morrison.

Tim quickly established a reputation as a crowd-pleaser. His smooth skating and headlong rushes thrilled many a Gardens crowd; before too long the Toronto media had

This is one of Tim's rookie photos. Tim would think his hair was long here; he was one of the last men to give up the crew cut. Of course nobody wore helmets then, so Tim had so many scars and scratches on his head, the crew cut made him look like a boxer.

Tim laying the body on New York Ranger tough guy, Lou Fontinato. With the Leafs Tim quickly gained a reputation as a tough but clean player.

IMPERIAL OIL LIMITED, TUROFSKY COLLECTION, HOCKEY HALL OF FAME

given him a new nickname — The Pony Express. Because of his strength Tim could always take care of himself on the ice. He quickly earned a reputation as a crushing body-checker — a tough but clean player who was nonetheless reluctant to fight. Tim was the first player to respond when a teammate was treated roughly, the first to step into a fray and separate players in a pile-up. If an opponent challenged him, or stepped out of line, Tim usually dealt with it by applying one of his trademark bear-hugs. A few seconds in Tim's iron grasp, or a quick body slam to the ice was usually enough to convince potential combatants they'd bitten off more than they could chew.

Tim would have to really lose it to drop his gloves, and the rare times that he did, he felt so bad about it afterwards, it would takes years before he would be involved in another fight. I can't remember it happening more than two or three times during his whole career. Tim got through his whole rookie season without getting involved in fighting (no mean feat for a rookie in any era), and it wasn't until Boxing Day of the following year that someone got him mad enough to earn a punch. With only six teams in the league, opposing players had ample opportunity to establish a real dislike for each other, and grudge matches were more common than they are today.

Tim had bragged two weeks earlier that he had been the only Leaf who avoided fisticuffs in a brawl with Montreal on December 9th, dubbed by the media as the "War of 1812" (because the fight broke out at 18:12 of the third period), but on this evening Red Wing forward Tony Leswick stepped well over the line, slashing Tim on the ankles on three separate occasions before Tim shed his gloves and dropped Leswick with a left hand.

Apart from his strength and skating ability, which set him apart from most NHL defensemen, Tim also acquired some notoriety for his "slap shot," which was still a novelty in the league at that time. Though Tim was not the first player to use it (Bill Barilko, for example, was known for his) he was one of handful of players — including Boom-Boom Geoffrion — who used it regularly.

One scary incident in Tim's first year was the time he nearly took Harry Lumley's ear off with a 45-footer during practice. Lumley's goaltending was a key reason the Leafs contended for the playoffs that year, and hearts stopped for a moment as the big Leaf goalie lay on the ice for a minute after the mishap. Lumley wasn't permanently damaged, though it did require five stitches to close the gash on his ear lobe. Once it became clear that their goalie would be all right, the wound provided an occasion for some dark

Tim developed a slap shot while playing in Pittsburgh, and even in his early years he had one of the hardest in the league. Though NHL players like Boom-Boom Geoffrion were already using it, the slap shot was still a relatively new development in the game in the early 1950s.

humour; a few of the Leafs had Primeau believing that Tim had taken off a piece of Lumley's ear, and sent the coach out on the ice to look for it.

Our first child, Jeri-Lynn, was born November 26th of Tim's rookie year. She was born very small — she wasn't quite five pounds at birth, so we were very concerned.

Tim and I with our first little angel, Jeri-Lynn, in our house on Warden Avenue. Don't you love the curtains? When Tim got word she was born he was playing a game in New York.

Jeri's lungs hadn't fully developed yet and she had problems taking her bottle, and I spent the first little while bugging some of the wives — particularly the very accommodating Jean Flaman — calling them up at all hours of the day and night begging for advice.

The day Jeri was born Tim was playing in New York. She was born at three in the afternoon and I woke him up from his pre-game sleep with the news. Tim sent his mother a telegram: "Delores's baby is born. Will you please go stay with her." He was so excited about having his first child that he couldn't concentrate on the game — Tim told me later that he was on for every goal-against that night. These days hockey players are given time off, and they are in the delivery room when their children are born, but Tim had to wait until the team got back into town before he had a free hour to come and see the baby. But nobody expected different in those days — that's

Tim, Jeri, and I at home. Jeri had a few physical problems in her early months, but as you can see, she caught up and became a very healthy baby.

just the way things were and Tim had warned me about this kind of thing plenty of times before we were married. He was a hockey player and things would be kind of different for us — he wouldn't be able to be there for me sometimes, and there would be times when I'd have to deal with these kinds of things by myself. In the end, it really wasn't all that bad, because the wives were all close and they were always in the background, always there for you. Wives and girlfriends used to spend the weekends together when the guys were out of town. We'd all take our babies over to Jean Flaman's house and play cards all night. I had a lot of good friends among the wives: Jean Flaman, Jean Sloan, June Smith, Lillian Watson . . . they were all great.

When the Leafs were in town we'd all go to the games together — we'd arrive with the team at six o'clock and we'd all go to the Honeydew, which was down the street — because the Gardens had no restaurant or anything like that — and we'd sit and talk for a good hour-and-a-half beforehand. I usually sat with Jean Sloan — her seats were always in the Blues, in Section 46 on the east side. Jean's seats weren't great — eventually Tim got me great hockey seats in Section 21, Row A, right above the goal. As wives we were always allowed two comps, so two of the girls would sit together and we took turns bringing a couple of friends down to watch a game.

In that first year, the Leafs faded in the second half of the season and missed the playoffs (as they did three out of Tim's first five years), done in by their love of the penalty box and key injuries to Max Bentley, Ted Kennedy, and George Armstrong. Tim wore 16 in his rookie season, but switched to number 7 at the request of King Clancy the

One of the first of
many appearances
for Tim on the cover
of the Gardens'
program. Note
the banners for the
original six teams.

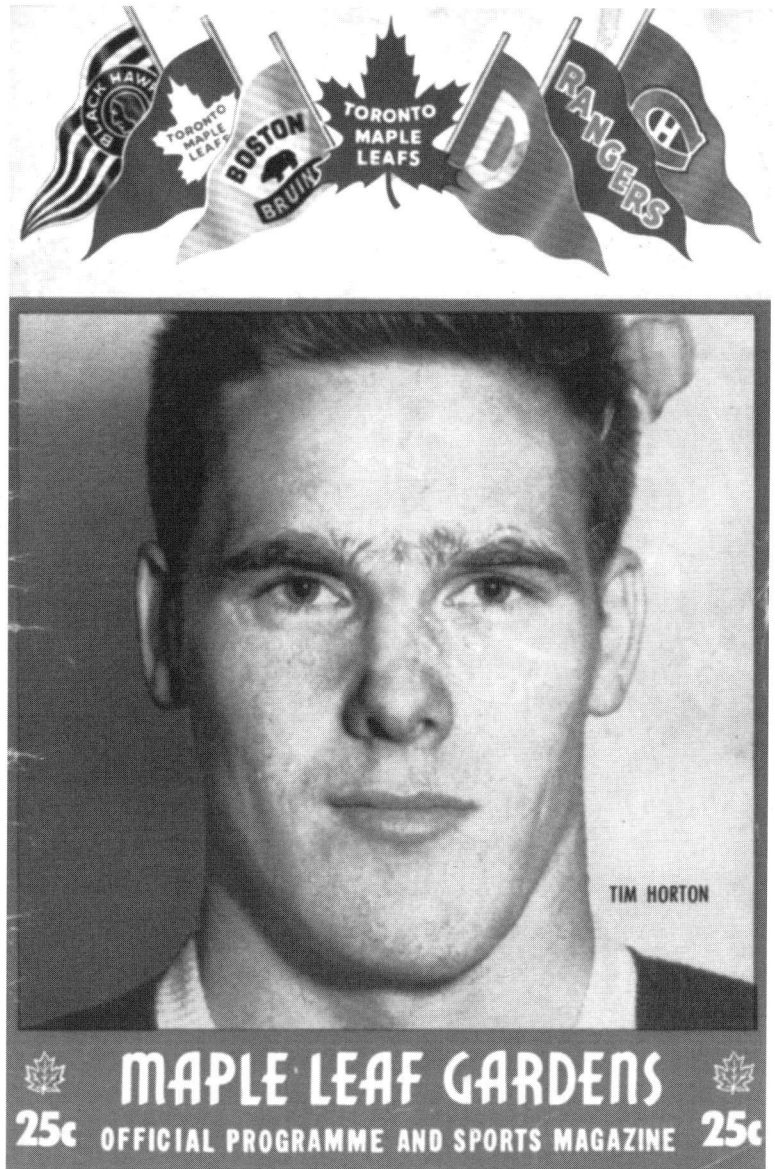

TIM HORTON

MAPLE·LEAF GARDENS
25¢ OFFICIAL PROGRAMME AND SPORTS MAGAZINE 25¢

following year. Tim considered it a great honour to wear the same number Clancy wore in his playing days.

One day, two or three years after Tim first moved up with the Leafs, he was told to stay by the phone because there was supposed to be a trade going through with Montreal. We stayed by the phone all afternoon, but nothing happened and we never heard another word about it. We'd been told it was a done deal, just a matter of them calling up and telling Tim where and when to report — we never really found out what had happened. At the time we weren't at all happy with the idea, but in retrospect I wonder how much better Tim might have done in Montreal. The Canadiens had a more offensive style than the

Tim and Jeri, about a year after she was born. Jeri was always
a classic "Daddy's Girl." When Tim used to leave each fall
for training camp, Jeri would run a fever and get sick to her
stomach. The doctor told us it was simply separation anxiety.

Leafs, and it might have been a better fit for the way he liked to play. By then we had two kids and just the thought of moving was enough to get us down.

The Leafs were in a transitional stage after the great teams of the late-1940s. Bill Barilko was gone. Babe Pratt had been traded; Bob Davidson, Nick Metz, and Syl Apps had all retired, and were followed in quick order by key Leafs the likes of Turk Broda, Howie Meeker, Gus Mortson, and captain Ted Kennedy. Star centre Max Bentley was sold to the Rangers after Tim's rookie season. And so, new coach King Clancy handled a team of mostly untested Leafs while they learned their trade through the mid-1950s. While Tim, George Armstrong, and Tod Sloan developed into front-line NHLers, the Leafs gradually added players such as Bobby Baun, Billy Harris, Bob Pulford, Dick Duff, Frank Mahovlich, and Dave Keon.

Duff was a St. Mike's star a few years after Tim graduated. He remembers the mid-1950s as rebuilding years for the Leafs: "After the 1951 Cup team was broken up, Tim and Army would have been the guys they were looking at. Tod Sloan was a little older but certainly one of their key players, Teeder Kennedy and Sid Smith were sort of on their way out. Even Jim Thomson was near the end of the line, so for two or three years we had a very young team. That may be why we bonded, because we just weren't a very good team at that point. But we developed a good team spirit as the team got better. There were always good young kids coming up, the system was always in place, we could see

Tim, Allan Stanley, and Don Simmons at a Leaf practice, early 1950s.
HOCKEY HALL OF FAME

that we were going to get better. Tim came out of St. Mike's in '49 or '50, Frank and I came a few years later, and a few years after that, Keon came."

TIM WAS ALWAYS AN extremely durable player — you'd have to be to play 23 seasons in the NHL. At one point in the 1960s, Tim played in 468 consecutive games for the Leafs, a team ironman record which remains unbroken. He only suffered one major injury during his NHL career, and it came late in 1956, during his fourth season with the Leafs.

In the second period of a home game against the New York Rangers, Tim was rushing up ice into the Rangers' zone. He had his head down as he crossed the blue line, and the Rangers' big defenseman Bill Gadsby met him head-on, at full speed. Tim always said that the check was a clean one, but Gadsby's shoulder caught Tim in the face, breaking his jaw, and Tim hit the ice like a ton of bricks. Landing awkwardly, Tim snapped his leg, just above the ankle.

I've talked to Bill several times in recent years and he still doesn't like to talk about that hit — he and his wife Edna felt awful about Bill being remembered as the one who broke Tim Horton's leg, and they felt worse when they

Tim and teammate Ron Stewart after Tim narrowly misses a goal against Chicago goalie Hank Bassen in a February, 1955 game. Chicago's Nick Mickoski (#9) is the Hawks defender.

IMPERIAL OIL LIMITED, TUROFSKY COLLECTION, HOCKEY HALL OF FAME

heard Tim's salary was cut the following season. Though at the time Gadsby described the check as the "hardest" he had "ever thrown," everyone who saw it knew it was really less of a body check than a collision. Tim chalked the whole thing up to bad luck — there was never any animosity toward Bill, who as far as Tim was concerned was just doing his job. In fact, Tim ultimately blamed the accident on the fact he'd polished all of his shoes that morning. Tim was very superstitious when it came to hockey, and he would never polish his shoes before a game again. It would be months, in fact, before Tim could even wear two shoes again.

Toronto Star article giving the details of Tim's injury in 1956, after a blind hit by New York's Bill Gadsby. It was an accident, really, and Gadsby still feels awful about being the guy who broke Tim's leg.
I was at the game, and you could hear the crack all through the Gardens.

Leafs' Cup Hopes Carried Out With Horton

By JIM PROUDFOOT

As the Maple Leafs' Tim Horton was carried off the Gardens' ice Saturday night with a broken leg and broken jaw, you couldn't help getting the idea that a large proportion of the home side's Stanley Cup hopes departed with him.

No player is indispensable, but it was obvious to 12,800 onlookers that Leafs weren't the same team without Horton. Before his injury occurred, late in the second period, they had been swarming all over their opponents—the also-ran New York Rangers—and only a series of "miracles" by New York goalie Gump Worsley had held Leafs to a 1-0 lead.

Perhaps stunned by Horton's accident, Leafs sleep-walked through the third period, particularly from a defensive standpoint, and blew a 2-1 decision to the Blueshirts.

Horton has been one of the Leafs' best, all through a mediocre season. He has been steady on defence and his spectacular dashes up the ice have lifted the team time and again. It was that led to his injury Saturday.

Tim had hit full speed as he crossed centre ice and seemed to have his head down as he passed the Ranger blue line. Defenceman Bill Gadsby of New York met him head-on and the collision sent Tim spinning. It was a clean check. Gadsby's shoulder seemed to catch Horton's face and the leg was twisted as he landed heavily. The shin bone of the right leg was fractured, as well as the lower jaw on the left side.

Gadsby said afterwards that, while he regretted it had resulted in an injury, it was "the best check I've ever thrown."

The game itself was a typically frustrating Leaf effort. They poured 36 shots at Worsley in the first two periods, while holding Rangers to 12, and had only a 1-0 lead to show for it.

Tod Sloan, who missed several good chances, the best being when he was set up in the clear by George Armstrong, finally beat Gump midway through the second. Army, playing the best game he's had at the Gardens this year, gave Parker McDonald a pass in front of the goal and, after Worsley made a fine stop, Sloan poked in the rebound.

The Rangers improved in the third, although neither of their goals was impressive. Both were long shots which most nights would be simple stops for Harry Lumley, although he may have been partially screened on them. Defenceman Lou Fontinato tied it early in the period and Pete

Conacher sank the winner. Danny Lewicki made the key pass on each occasion.

The McDonald - Armstrong - Sloan line was very good for Leafs and must have had half of the Toronto shots on goal. Sloan and Armstrong were robbed of at least two sure goals each by Worsley.

Larry Cahan checked with authority and moved around well. Only blotch on a fine record was a rather senseless interference penalty in the last

minutes of the game when Leafs might have been going after the tying goal.

Rangers were outclassed in every department, except the one that goes into the record book.

Notes: Bill McCreary, a Sundridge, Ont. boy, signed a pro contract with Rangers Saturday and played his first full-fledged NHL game. A veteran of four years of junior hockey in Guelph, he had already used up his three-game amateur tryout . . . Edgar Laprade, retiring after 10 sea-

sons with Rangers, was saying "so long" to his teammates. He's returning to Port Arthur and his sporting goods business. He may have a try at amateur hockey.

Leafs used Varsity Blues' Paul Knox and he played a sound game. He worked at right wing with Ted Kennedy and Sid Smith . . . Joe Klukay suffered a badly bruised left arm when he was speared by Worsley's stick . . . The three-star selection read Worsley, Sloan, Don Raleigh.

HORTON, JUST BEFORE HE WAS HIT

I was in the stands as usual that night and I knew something was wrong right away — everyone did — you could hear the crack of the leg breaking all around the rink and Tim's leg was at a sickening angle, so there was no mistaking what had happened. When I saw Tim lying there I couldn't move; I was really in shock. I sat there dumbfounded until an usher came for me and took me down to the dressing room.

Dick Duff was also in the Gardens that night. He was a Junior star at that point, close to signing with the Leafs, and was sitting up in the box with Conn Smythe. "I was just coming up out

HORTON'S WIFE VISITS HIM IN HOSPITAL

—Star Photo by Frank Teskey

Tim Horton's pretty wife was one of the few persons to see him yesterday in Toronto East General hospital, where he is bedded down with a broken leg and fractured jaw, result of an accident in Saturday night's hockey game at the Gardens

Visiting Tim in Toronto East General hospital, a day or two after his injury. Because his jaw was broken, the doctors had to extract a tooth so they could feed him through a straw. It was the first tooth Tim had lost playing hockey.

FRANK TESKEY, TORONTO STAR

of Junior and I saw what happened to Timmy," Duff remembers, "and I realized right away that this was going to be a serious business that I was going to get involved in. I mean, there wasn't even a penalty on that play — it just happened with the speed he was going and the way he hit the ice." In the Greens, in one of two seats Smythe reserved for St. Mike's players, a youthful Frank Mahovlich also watched the accident:

"Tim was the only player who could really carry the puck for Toronto in those days. If they needed to get the puck out of their end, he was the guy. He was skating fast and going from one foot to the other. He must have had his head down because Gadsby caught him just right, and you could hear the snap all over the rink. I was up in the Greens and I could hear it very clearly. And the next day in the paper they were saying spiral break of the leg and broken jaw. It was amazing the way he came back from that."

Tim's face was swelling up as they were loading him into an ambulance to take him to the hospital. He had a compound fracture of his leg just above the ankle, and you could see the bone sticking through as he lay there on the stretcher. Tim was in pain, but alert, and what he was most concerned with at the time was which hospital they were going to take him to. They wanted to take him to Wellesley but he wanted to go to East General because it was closer to home. By the time we got to hospital his face was badly swollen, and I was getting concerned, so I removed Tim's contact lenses before his eye swelled shut.

55

Leaf trainer Tim
Daly examines
Tim's leg after the
cast is removed.
It took a long time
(almost two years)
for Tim to fully
recover from the
injury. The muscle
had completely
deteriorated while
the cast was on, and
Tim had to rebuild
the strength in his
right leg.

T IM WAS IN HOSPITAL for a good month while his jaw
healed. That was where he lost his first tooth — they
had to pull one so they could feed him because his mouth was
wired shut. Tim had a few bad weeks, but then he was up in
a wheelchair visiting everybody on the floor.

It was a long hard road back for Tim from that injury.
Tim's leg was broken in March and he was in a full cast, up
to his hip, until July. So when the cast came off, the muscle
had completely deteriorated — all that was left was skin
and bone. It was a bad injury, and Tim had some serious
doubts at one point whether he'd ever be able to play
hockey again.

It was during that summer that Tim first met Bobby Baun,
who was still with the Marlies, but would come up and join
the Leafs the next season. It was Bobby who helped Tim get
back into shape. Tim had been given a job in a gravel pit
owned by Connie Smythe.

Baun remembers it this way:

"The first time I met Timmy was at the sand and gravel pit that Smythe owned. Tim was looking after the scales, waving the trucks in and out. I became Tim's gopher for that summer, and, I tell you, he kept me on the run. I also met Lori and the kids and I started doing some baby-sitting for the Hortons as well."

"It couldn't have been much fun for Tim, but I remember it as a great summer. After he got the cast off we started working out at the 'Y' — we would hobble around the track together with me leading him around. Tim was still hurting at that time, so he never really wanted to do it. After a while we started playing some basketball and doing a lot of swimming. Gradually, we started going to Ted Reeve arena [on Main Street and Gerrard, in the east end, where the Leafs used to practise] — just by ourselves. Tim could still hardly skate at that point. It was a tough time for him but I think that really was when our friendship grew, so I have good memories of that summer. We worked and we worked and finally Tim started going with the weights and that. But it was probably about a year before he started to feel half-decent again."

Though Smythe had given Tim a job while he was recovering, the Leafs brass were not exactly supportive of Tim through this whole period. He had his pay cut by $500 the next year for time missed, and when he did start playing again, he was fined $100 by GM Hap Day for what he referred to as "indifferent play." It took a long time even then for the muscles in the injured leg to build up so it was the same size as the other leg, and Tim limped for quite a while in the meantime. Years after Tim recovered he'd still have trouble with it sometimes on rainy days.

One of the only good things about the injury was that for a time Tim got to see a lot of his family. Our second girl, Kim, was born May 21, 1955, just a few weeks after Tim was released from hospital. When Tim took me in to the same hospital for the delivery, there was some confusion about who it was who needed the wheelchair: Tim, with his cast and crutches trying to juggle me and my suitcases, or me, doubled over in pain.

Our third girl, Kelly, was born the following September. We were still living on Warden Avenue through this

Here Tim has his hands full with Jeri and the new baby, Kim, who was born while Tim's leg was still in a cast. The girl at the top of the picture is a neighbour.

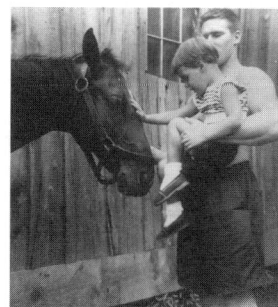

This is a picture of a nice trip we made with our next-door neighbours down to a farm just south of Erie, Pennsylvania. That's Jeri petting the horse with Tim.

57

Tim, still with a cast, just after he got home from the hospital. We had kind of an open house when we lived on Warden; I never knew who Tim would bring home for dinner. The guy on the right of the picture is Barney, someone Tim met while in hospital.

period. Tim's teammates Ray Timgren, Ron Stewart (and his wife Barbara), and the Griggs's all lived within a few blocks and the Griggs would become our Toronto family. Suburbia at that time was out on the edge of farm country. But playing for the Leafs Tim still became something of a local celebrity. When we moved in, the two little boys next door, Jack and Kenny Conway, were in Thistletown Hospital with polio. The boys' parents Dave and Sheila still credit Tim moving in next door with getting them well — the two of them couldn't get home fast enough to meet him.

There were nine houses on our block and we were all close — the families used to get together and have parties and whenever anything needed doing, whether it was a fence

58

Shift Sid Smith

Horton Practices With Maple Leafs For First Time

By AL NICKLESON

Tim Horton experimented with a leg, and the Maple Leafs with some bodies yesterday. Both trial runs merged into something of a success although true proving grounds lie in actual league combat.

While the Leafs juggled some forwards—notably All-Star Sid Smith — defenseman Horton scrimmaged with the team for the first time since a leg break last March. He had been test-skating the injury daily since fall training period, but always solo.

"I tried to work just like in a game," said Horton. "The leg didn't bother me a bit."

Whether the Pony Express will make his seasonal National Hockey League debut against the front-running Montreal Canadiens here tomorrow night hasn't been decided. General Manager Hap Day may venture on the subject following today's team prep.

Certainly, Horton's end-to-end rushes and general defensive ability have been missed. But it won't all come back at once. Yesterday, he drove hard but he lacked condition and timing after such a long absence. His efforts, however, pleased the brass.

"We'll decide later about Tim playing Wednesday," said Day. "There's quite a difference between a practise and a game."

Up front, Day and Coach King Clancy shifted left-winger Smith onto a line with centre Rudy Migay and right-winger Ron Stewart. Smith had been playing with freshman centre Billy Harris, the kid from Marlboro juniors of last season, and Eric Nesterenko.

In winning an NHL all-star berth last spring, Smith emerged with 33 goals and 21 assists. This season, undoubtedly missing the retired Ted Kennedy at centre, he has been held goalless and to three assists in eight games.

The fault rests with neither Harris nor Smith, but rather in their somewhat-conflicting styles of play. Harris, especially, has been a crowd-pleaser and is regarded as certain to stick in the big-time.

A newspaper clipping which appeared after Tim returned to the Leafs. This was the first time Tim practised with his teammates after coming back from the injury, but he had already logged a lot of rehabilitation working out all summer with Bobby Baun at Ted Reeve Arena in Toronto's east end.

TORONTO STAR

which had to go up or some project like that, all the guys would get together and pitch in.

We met Dennis Griggs when he asked Tim to be his assistant coach on a local boys' baseball team. The kids were all around 12 and Ed Griggs was one of the players. Under Tim and Dennis's careful guidance, the team won exactly one game all year — still everyone had a great time and we ended the year with a barbecue at our house. Gord Griggs was delivering for the local drugstore at that time, but he would later attend Knox College and go on to become a Presbyterian minister. Gord would play a large part in all of our lives.

Tim rushes to cover
the front of the net
after Leafs' goalie Ed
Chadwick makes a save
off a sprawling Camille
Henry in a January,
1959, home game
against the Rangers.
Larry Popein is
standing in the slot.
Ron Stewart looks
on as a young Eddie
Shack jams the crease
for the Rangers.

IMPERIAL OIL LIMITED,
TUROFSKY COLLECTION,
HOCKEY HALL OF FAME

Gord remembers Tim as a very solid, down-to-earth person who was very interested in spiritual matters. "We thought alike in terms of people. In terms of what was important," he recalls. "When he heard that I was going back to school to become a minister, he was very interested in that. We talked a lot about all sorts of things. Tim was a very special person in terms of his understanding of God. He never pretended to have all the answers. And he displayed on the ice the image of a very hard-working man, who did his job, and didn't draw attention to himself. That's who he was."

This is one of my favorite
photos; Gordie Hannigan
and Tim mugging it up
while feeding the babies.
Gordie and his wife
Anne lived in the west
end when Hurricane
Hazel hit in 1956. They
came to live with us for
a couple of months until
the damage to their
house was repaired.

Our dog, Punchy, a beautiful, intelligent collie, took over the job of protecting the block. The neighbours would feed her, much to my dismay; after fried liver from the house down the street she would turn her nose up at the dog food I would put out for her. Occasionally she would decide to "visit" a nearby sheep farm and do what her breed had been meant to do: "herd the sheep." We were really out in farm country at that time. Eventually the owner threatened to shoot her if we didn't keep the dog at home. At times Punchy seemed to be more than just smart. Our baby sitter was completely spooked the night Tim broke his leg when the dog started howling and could not be comforted.

One of Tim's best friends on the Leafs was Gord Hannigan, who he'd known from when he started at St. Mike's. Gord was one of three brothers connected with the Leafs; all three played with the big club at one time or another.

Here's a family shot in our living room on Wedgewood Avenue. Kim's still a baby, and that's our dog Punchy who had just had a bath (and who was not named after Punch Imlach).

IMPERIAL OIL LIMITED,
TUROFSKY COLLECTION,
HOCKEY HALL OF FAME

**Tim changing Traci
on that same couch.
You can see that Jeri
is already getting
tall. Tim was a
pretty liberated guy,
looking back on it.
He was never above
helping out around
the house.**

Ray scored the Calder Cup-winning overtime goal with
Tim in Pittsburgh, Gord was a star in the AHL and started
his rookie NHL season with a bang, but could never match
that initial success. Pat, the youngest of the three, played
only one game with Toronto, and was one of the players
involved in the trade which brought Eddie Shack to the
Leafs in 1960. He was with New York during the 1962
Stanley Cup finals between the Rangers and the Leafs.
Gord was a close friend of Tim's for years. It was a blow to
us both when, in 1966, he died of a heart attack at the age
of 37.

Gordie and his wife Anne lived out in the west end in the
summer of 1956 when Hurricane Hazel blew in. When the
hurricane hit, the house they were living in was flooded,
and they came to live with us while it was being repaired.
One of my favourite photos is of Gordie and Tim mugging
it up for the camera while feeding the babies. Gord and
Anne had nine kids together. In the end, I think that's

This is Kimmy after her christening.

Another shot of Tim and the girls while Kim is still a baby. The one good thing about Tim's injury was that he got to see a lot of his kids that summer.

why Gord stopped playing hockey — he couldn't afford it; he had too many kids to raise. Gord eventually joined his brother Ray in Edmonton in the drive-in restaurant business.

Tim was always good around the house. He did dishes and changed diapers, and he particularly enjoyed putting the kids to bed. After the kids were bathed and in their pyjamas he would lead a parade of three little ones singing "We are Marching to Pretoria," as he tucked each one of them in. Corny, I know, but it was his favourite part of the day.

Tim was making a decent living as a player through these years, but with a house and family he still couldn't afford to take the summers off. During the first couple of years, we went back to North Bay for the summer and Tim kept his job lugging beer for the Brewer's Retail. Later, Tim worked at a variety of jobs — he sold ads for the *Toronto Star*, he was even in real estate for one year — and did very well at it, actually. He'd gotten his licence the year he broke his leg on the assumption that he might never play hockey again, but when he returned to the Leafs the licence lapsed.

Jeri's second birthday party at Warden. We were very close with the neighbours on our block. Our kids would play together, and if a fence had to go up, all the guys would pitch in and do it together.

This is an Easter Sunday after church. We now have three girls; I'm holding Kelly, who was born the previous September. This is the front lawn of our house in Scarborough, and believe it or not, that's Warden Avenue behind us.

Tim, the girls, and his mother, Ethel. You can see that he does look quite a bit like his mother. Ethel said Tim looked a lot like *her* Dad. Ethel also came from a family of four daughters.

Tim cleaning one of his cars — it looks like another Mercury. Tim used to wear that kind of hat all the time, especially when he was driving his sports cars. For some reason he thought he looked sharp.

A few summers later, Tim got involved with his first business venture, a hamburger place which was started up by his brother Gerry up in North Bay which they called "The Big Seven." Tim provided most of the financing, and the business ran for several years and did modestly well, but I found the schedule a little difficult. Tim's father owned a garage on the same property and we would drive up every weekend in the summer to check on the businesses. The kids loved it. Grandma would have a selection of homemade pies ready, and they had their cousins to play with; they have nothing but fond memories of North Bay. We did this for several years. I would pack up the kids and the dog in the car and we'd travel with all the weekend traffic. We rarely saw Tim on the weekend; Tim would spend all day with his brother and father at the garage or the restaurant and the kids and I would go to the beach. In retrospect I think I put up with this a lot longer than I should have.

64

This is the hamburger place started by Gerry up in North Bay. Tim provided a lot of the financing. Despite having three kids to transport we spent every weekend up in North Bay, and while the girls loved spending time with their grandmother, all that driving was a grind after a while.

A rare moment of relaxation for Tim up in North Bay in Gerry's back yard. Tim would spend most of his weekends dealing with the business and I'd take the girls out to the beach at Lake Nippissing.

I would go up every weekend without a peep. But it did have its drawbacks; for years Tim's mother thought I didn't like her because I'd be in such a bad mood when we got there. Life was tough enough taking care of three kids and, in the end, it was too much for everyone to make that long trip every weekend.

Tam Horton

Tim in the mid-1950s, by then a fixture for the Leafs. Tim was always an excellent skater, and became very good in his own end, but he always felt he was never allowed to play his own game in Toronto — he was most effective when he rushed the puck and joined the offence.

AT THE END OF THE 1955–56 season King Clancy switched jobs with the Leafs from coach to assistant general manager. The Leafs' management was in disarray during the mid-1950s, despite the fact they were gradually stockpiling what would prove to be an exceptional group of players. Dick Duff had been a strong candidate for rookie-of-the-year in 1955–56 (he lost out to Chicago goalie Glenn Hall) and fellow St. Mike's alumnus Frank Mahovlich would actually win the Calder Trophy the following season.

Howie Meeker replaced Clancy as coach for that year, during the majority of which Tim was sidelined with his leg injury. In the off-season Meeker was offered the General Manager's job, took it, then was quickly dismissed by Staf-

ford Smythe, Conn's son, who was gradually taking a larger part in the running of the hockey team. Billy Reay became the new Leafs' coach.

King, an offensive force from the blue line in his own playing days, was always a big fan of Tim's style of play — more than once comparing him to Detroit Red Wings great Red Kelly, although like all of Tim's coaches Clancy felt he never took full advantage of his hard shot.

Billy Reay was a different story. It took Tim a year-and-a-half to get his game back to where it had been before his injury, but his cause wasn't helped much by his new coach, who benched him for long periods during the '57–'58 season. I don't know whether it was Tim's style of play he didn't like, or Tim himself, but Tim hated playing for Reay and always felt Billy just had it in for him.

I remember one time during that year Tim had the Asian flu, and he was in bed with a temperature of 104. Hugh Smythe, the team doctor, came out to the house to see him and he said, "Tim, I don't know what to tell you, but Billy

Tim clearing the net in front of Leafs' goalie Harry Lumley. The Leaf teams of the early and mid-1950s, despite stellar goaltending from the likes of Lumley and Chadwick, languished near the bottom of the standings. The team's fortunes didn't really change until the arrival of Punch Imlach.

IMPERIAL OIL LIMITED, TUROFSKY COLLECTION, HOCKEY HALL OF FAME

67

This is Tim visiting my nephew D.J. at the Air Force academy in Colorado during one of the Leafs' pre-season tours. D.J. was just a cadet at this point.

Tim on one of his many promotional gigs, presenting a plaque to a youngster. The players used to get paid $25 for a personal appearance, but then the Gardens would take $10 back. Compare that to what goes on nowadays.

insists that you play tonight." Tim had been benched earlier in the year and he didn't want it to happen again, so he got himself out of bed, went down and played the hockey game, ended up one of the three stars, then he came home and damned near died. It was a decision that should have been up to the team doctor, but obviously it wasn't. After Tim got better, he returned to the team and he was benched for another two weeks. That was what it was like playing for Reay.

I never met the man, but obviously Reay wasn't Tim's favourite person in the world. The team did poorly under him, and when George "Punch" Imlach was hired later that summer as assistant general manager, fired Reay, and took over behind the bench early in the new season, we were both pretty happy. Billy Reay did the Leafs at least one important service, though, during his tenure with the club. After coaching in the American League championships the previous year, and losing to the Cleveland Barons, he recommended that the Leafs acquire the Barons' goalie who backstopped the victory — a smallish, veteran goalie named Johnny Bower who'd been languishing in the American League for years.

B ECAUSE OF ALL HIS problems under Reay, for Tim, Punch Imlach's hiring was like the arrival of the Messiah, though that wasn't the case for all of the players. Punch was

Tim as he looked in the late 1950s. Tim weathered some dark days under coach Billy Reay. He was benched for long stretches of the 1957–58 season, and for some reason Tim never could get out of Reay's doghouse. Reay was the only coach who Tim played for that he actually disliked.

HOCKEY HALL OF FAME

Punch Imlach, with his trademark felt hat, behind the
Maple Leafs' bench. Both the Leafs and Tim thrived under
Imlach. Both Joe Primeau and King Clancy were players'
coaches. According to Tim, Punch was the exact opposite:
"If he had stopped screaming, we'd have gone for the doctor."

Leafs' Horton Feels Happier
And His Hockey Is Snappier
Under New Gardens Regime

By RED BURNETT

George "Punch" Imlach, who is doubling in brass as the Leaf general manager and coach, is the best thing that has happened to Tim Horton, in a hockey sense, since Tim made the second NHL all-star team in 1953-54.

When Imlach took over as coach, Tim was listed as trade bait. In the past five games, he has been one of the most solid performers in the Toronto lineup.

Right now he looks like the Horton of old, the dashing defender who lifted fans out of their seats with his length-of-the-ice rushes and solid blocking.

Tim, who has been in and out of the Leaf doghouse ever since he suffered a fractured jaw and fractured leg after taking a crushing check from Ranger defenceman Bill Gadsby late in the 1954-55 season, credits Imlach with his return to form.

"Imlach knows what he wants and has a knack of getting his ideas across to the player," Horton says. "What's even more important is that he makes you feel you are capable of carrying out his instructions.

"Now, I don't worry about making mistakes. I know Imlach will pull me off the ice, correct the error and send me back into action. There's no danger of being shunted to the end of the bench without being told why.

"When Imlach took over as coach he had

us all in for private sessions before the team meeting. He gave us a chance to air our gripes.

"I had been instructed to pass the puck as soon as I got it in our zone. I like to carry that puck, have a good look before I pass it.

"Imlach instructed me to do so. Now, I'm looking forward to every shift on the ice instead of worrying about the possibility of making mistakes.

"Having Allan Stanley on the left side is also a big help. Allan is one of the steadiest in the league. You always know where he is and can count on him to back you up in the clutch."

At the moment, it's doubtful you could pry Horton loose via the trade route.

One of the main reasons for the team's improved "goals against" record—six in their last four games—has been the play of the defence. Horton and Stanley have played the leading roles.

Horton's effort in Montreal as Leafs tied Canadiens, 2-2, was one of his top performances as a Leaf. It was reminiscent of his work in 1953-54.

Tim is moving with more assurance and has better puck control. He has steadied away and is making the attacker move before committing himself.

Four games don't make a season but Tim could be on the way back as a top-notch defenceman.

always a guy who, as far as the players were concerned, you either loved or hated. Combining the roles of coach and general manager has always been an awkward business, but never more so than with the penny-pinching Leafs of the late 1950s and early 1960s.

In his book about the Leaf teams of that decade, *The Glory Years*, Tim's teammate Billy Harris describes Punch's contradictory role in a nutshell:

"Negotiating your contract, [Punch] would attempt to sign you for the least amount possible, and to do so he would remind you of your shortcomings as a hockey player. . . . No Leaf ever became wealthy under Imlach. Players who were married and had children really had no bargaining power and generally signed for what they were offered. Most of us

When Imlach took over, the first thing he did was loosen the restrictions on Tim's rushing. This, and the acquisition of veteran Allan Stanley from Boston, rejuvenated Tim and the whole Leafs' defense. The press (as in this *Star* article) were quick to recognize the change in atmosphere.

71

were living in Toronto and preferred not to move elsewhere. But after Punch in his role of general manager had denigrated us all and signed everyone as cheaply as possible, he then as a coach had to convince us we were good hockey players and a great team and could beat all our opponents."

"The ownership of the Leafs was brutal in those days," Mahovlich recalls. These were the days before agents came

Tim on the bench, late 1950s. With Imlach in charge, Tim became a key player on what would soon become a Stanley Cup contender.

MAPLE LEAF GARDENS

on the scene. Players would negotiate their own contracts with owners who made them feel like they were doing them a favour letting them play in the NHL. "The way it was orchestrated, and the whole structure, the way things worked, in that era was really tough on players. I don't know how we did it. Allan Stanley used to say that we'd win championships in spite of them. And then when we won it, they'd get all the credit, so we wondered if we made a mistake."

Over the next couple of years, Punch would build one of the best teams in NHL history. But with the rest of the Leafs' management, he would also help build up resentments among the players that would prove to be the undoing of the franchise in future years. The Leafs were not the only

Tim horsing around with the kids at home. Tim would lay down to have nap and one of the girls would yell, "Daddy wants to play!" Then they'd all pile on.

team to play hardball with its players in those years — Detroit's treatment of star players Ted Lindsay and Gordie Howe may be the most shameful of such examples — but they were certainly the most consistent.

Punch may have played the villain in most of these contract negotiations, but there was no denying his hockey abilities. In terms of assessing and acquiring players, as a general manager Punch was nothing short of brilliant. As far as coaching was concerned, Tim always preferred Joe Primeau; still Punch knew how to handle his players and had a knack for getting the most out of them.

"When Punch came to Toronto in '58, it was a real boost," Mahovlich remembers. "Everyone started playing 10% or 15% better than they ever had before." Not that the Leafs' transformation happened overnight. In *The Glory Years*, Billy Harris recalls Imlach holding individual meetings with the players so they could air their gripes, and so he could pass on the message that if they all pulled together, they could "turn this thing around." At the time, Punch might have been the only member of the team who thought so. The Leafs had started horribly under Reay, and well into

For ten years, Tim never ate a meal without a baby on his knee. Tim liked holding them, and when he was at home, there was always at least one there with him. In this picture, it's Traci.

March were showing little under Imlach that would convince you they were a playoff team.

With five games left in the season — fresh off a string of only three wins in 11 games — the Leafs' situation looked hopeless. They were still seven points out of a playoff spot, and even if they won all of their remaining games they would require help from other teams if they were to have any chance at all of squeezing in. With a loss or a tie meaning elimination, the Leafs' top forwards — Mahovlich, Armstrong, and Duff — came out of the doldrums as Toronto beat the Rangers in a home-and-home series to start the streak. The sweep left the Leafs three points behind with three games to play.

A few nights later, the Bruins did the Leafs a service, handing the Rangers their third straight loss a day before the Leafs went into Montreal to play the mighty Canadiens. Taking advantage of the absence of Canadiens goalie

Jacques Plante, and more scoring heroics from Dicky Duff — always a fantastic pressure player — the Leafs won 6–3 to stay alive.

Punch came back into the picture before the Leafs' last two games against Chicago and Detroit. The team was scheduled to travel to Detroit after that evening's game against the Blackhawks. At the team meeting Imlach told the players to pack enough clothes for a week — after wins over Chicago and Detroit, he reasoned, the team would have to go straight to Boston to start the playoffs. The request which seemed all the more ridiculous when the Rangers beat Detroit to pull ahead three points with two to play, but Punch's confidence stirred the players again. The Leafs beat Chicago 5–1, and had come back to tie the Red Wings 4–4 in the second period of the final game when the players heard over the PA system that the Canadiens had beaten New York in their final game of the year. The Leafs won a nail-biter with third period goals from Duff and Harris, capping off perhaps the most remarkable late-season charge in NHL history.

The Leafs' comeback to make the playoffs in 1959 is still referred to as "The Miracle Finish." The Leafs beat the Bruins that year in the semi-finals, but lost to Montreal in five games in the Stanley Cup finals. Still, most Toronto players from that era remember that spring as the year the Maple Leafs turned things around.

Tim's best years were still ahead of him, and his first Stanley Cup was still three years away, but when he was asked in later years to identify his biggest thrill, Tim would always point to those few games in the spring of 1959 as the most fun he ever had playing hockey.

Tim with his full complement of daughters. That's Jeri with the funny glasses. Both she and the baby, Traci, inherited Tim's bad eyesight, unfortunately. That's Kelly with the stuffed toy, and Kim on the right.

Tim, now a Leaf veteran, dressed for battle, circa 1965. The picture says it all.

FRANK PRAZAK/HOCKEY HALL OF FAME

III

'Tiger'

We were arguing back and forth, in a joking sort of way,
and Tim and Allan opened the window on the second
floor. And they both grabbed me by one leg and dangled
me out the window, saying: "How do you feel about the
defensive team now, Dicky?"

— *Dicky Duff*

AFTER THE MIRACLE FINISH of 1959, Punch Imlach set
about reinventing the Leafs as Stanley Cup contenders.
Players like Tim, Dick Duff, and George Armstrong were just
coming into their prime, and the Leafs had more than their

Tim with Red Kelly,
1962. Red, who
had won four
Stanley Cups with
the Red Wings as
a defenseman,
was considering
retirement when
Imlach plucked
him from Detroit
to play centre for
the Leafs. He'd go
on to win four more
Cups with Toronto.
BILLY HARRIS

Johnny Bower after a save against the Rangers. Allan Stanley clears the puck while Tim covers his man in the corner. That's Andy Bathgate, a future Leafs' teammate, against the far boards behind Stanley.
GRAPHIC ARTISTS/
HOCKEY HALL OF FAME

share of talented youngsters, so Imlach's job was mostly a matter of adding some good, experienced veterans.

One of the things Punch had a knack for was recognizing veteran players whose careers would benefit from a change of scenery. When Detroit star defenseman Red Kelly refused a trade to New York and appeared on the verge of retiring, Punch grabbed him off the Red Wings for young defenseman Marc Reaume. Kelly had been the premier offensive defenseman of his day, and one of the big reasons (the others were named Orr and Harvey) why Tim never won the Norris Trophy. Imlach had an idea that Kelly might make a good centreman. I guess he was right.

There was some dispute about Johnny Bower's age when he joined the Leafs in the middle of the 1958–59 season. His date of birth is listed as November 8, 1924, which would have made him 34 at that point. Bower had spent years in the minors on an excellent Cleveland Barons team, so when he first made it with the Leafs he might have exaggerated how old he was. At any rate, he told everyone he was 39. Johnny played another ten years with the Leafs. He was the number one goalie for the first few years; later he shared duties with Terry Sawchuk. But Johnny stayed "39" well into the 1960s. I remember the time some us met Jack Benny — he was in town playing at the O'Keefe

Centre. Benny used to have the same joke — he'd tell everyone he was "39" — and that was the first thing Benny said when he met us: "I hear you guys have a goaltender my age."

PUNCH HAD ACQUIRED veteran defenseman Allan Stanley from the Bruins in October, 1958, and by the following season Stanley and Tim had become one of the best defensive tandems in the NHL. "Tim was always a good hockey player," Armstrong believes, "but he really became a *great* player when he and Al started playing together."

Allan recalls his first few weeks with the Leafs:

"When I first went to Toronto in 1958, the first two weeks Baun and I played together. Tim was playing with Carl Brewer. After two weeks they switched us over and Tim and I started playing together, and that's the way it stayed. We just seemed to fit right in. It's not often that you play with somebody and are able to have that kind of confidence in him. Tim and I used to talk hockey a lot."

"I think I might have been the more offensive player for the first while. But Tim got tired of that quickly and began rushing more. There was one incident I remember in particular. One of us must have gotten caught up the ice once or twice early in the game, because Punch came into the dressing room between periods and gave us hell, telling us we were defensemen and were supposed to hang back. Tim and I went out on our next shift, I forget who we were playing, but they came down the ice on us. Tim and I always played right at the blue line. Their centreman tried to pull something funny, the two wingers had already gone in, and I kicked the puck away from him with my feet and started up ice."

"I got to the red line and I could hear someone coming up behind me, so I look over my shoulder and I see Tim. But just as I'm seeing Tim I'm also seeing our bench, and Punch is up on the bench with one foot on the boards and his hat off, getting all red. But Tim just kept coming. He charged right through the middle of their defense, and as he did I dumped the puck in to him. He went through, picked up the puck, and put it in the net."

"After the period Tim and I are sitting in the dressing room, and Punch comes straight over to us. 'I thought I told

Allan Stanley with
Gerry Ehman (Mark
and Jane Rheame are
in back) at a Christmas
party at our house,
early 1960s. Allan's
nickname was "Sam,"
a name he adopted
after no one seemed
to be able to spell his
name properly. Allan
and Tim clicked right
away, on and off the
ice. "Tim was always
a good hockey player,
but he really became
a *great* player when
he and Al started
playing together."
(George Armstrong)
AUTHORS' COLLECTION

you bastards not to play up ice,' he says. And I told him this was different because when I saw Timmy coming up there I *knew* he was going to get a goal. Punch just shook his head, turned around, and walked out of the room."

In the end, Allan became more of a stay-at-home type of defenseman, allowing Tim more room to rush up ice with the offense. The two just seemed to be made for each other — Allan covering when Tim got caught up ice, and Tim backing Allan up on opposition rushes:

"Tim and I developed our own different style of play," Stanley remembers. "I used to line up right on the blue line, or sometimes ten feet inside. But of course as a defenseman you can't be up there and back in the corner too. So Tim would be over in my corner a lot. I remember telling Tim I thought it was a tough way to play, standing that far out, because some of these guys were real skaters. I said, 'It doesn't bother me when they go to the outside; I can handle that. But I'm always afraid they'll cut into the middle.' And Tim said, 'Al, if they cut into the middle I've got them, so don't worry about it.' And I never worried about it again. It didn't matter who they were, or where they decided to cut in, Tim always had them covered."

80

Though Tim was the swifter skater of the two, Allan did his share of covering as well. Tim's trouble with his eyes hadn't got any better, and after the big injury, he wouldn't wear the contacts either. I'm not sure why he didn't just wear glasses; he wore them all the time off the ice. But nobody wore glasses in those days; Al Arbour wore them, but I don't remember anyone else. It's a good thing Allan Stanley was an excellent passer.

"I remember one time I asked Tim, where is your favourite spot to receive a pass?" Stanley recalls. "And Tim said: 'Allan, I'm going to put my stick down, and if you don't hit it, I'm not going to see it.'"

Throughout his career, Tim would need directions on certain pucks when they were thrown into the corner behind him, and he had particular trouble on plays where the puck got caught up in his feet. On plays where he couldn't find the puck at all, Tim's usual trick was just to knock down the man in front of him, the logic being that an opponent couldn't do much from the seat of his pants.

Frank Mahovlich and his wife Marie, at the same party. Perhaps it was because they were also St. Mike's alumni, or because they were offensive stars, but when it came to playing pranks, Tim got a special pleasure out of victimizing Frank and Dicky Duff.

AUTHORS' COLLECTION

George Armstrong once joked that Tim "was good at everything except seeing." I often wonder how good Tim could have been if his eyesight hadn't been so bad. On defense, he made up for any disadvantage he had with instinct, strength, and skating ability. But on offense, better eyesight would almost certainly have meant more goals.

Frank Mahovlich tells a story about a close encounter in New York with one of Tim's slapshots:

"I remember Gump Worsley was in net. I was going in and I wasn't looking where I was going and their defenseman comes up and really hits me. I mean I was lying face down, my stick went flying, and I was spread-eagled on the ice. I didn't know where the puck was, and I looked up and I could see Tim. He had the puck at the blue line and he was winding up to slap it. I was down on the ice thinking what am I going to do — he's gonna kill me. He was going to shoot at the net, and I was in front of the net, and he didn't see me. But God must have been on my side because he missed the shot."

"My stick was about ten feet away, and the puck goes way wide, hits my stick, and then goes in the net. Worsley was amazed. I got up and Worsley looked at me, and I looked at Worsley. Then he started swearing, and I just put up my hands, like, 'Don't blame me, I had nothing to do with it.' And talk about luck, I got credit for the goal."

As a team, the Leafs improved immensely over the next two seasons, but they were not yet ready to challenge the mighty Canadiens, at that time led by Jean Beliveau, Boom-Boom Geoffrion, and Jacques Plante. The Canadiens would win an unprecedented five straight Stanley Cups in the late 1950s and early '60s.

Imlach continued his tinkering, adding role players Eddie Shack and winger Bert Olmstead, a ferocious competitor from small-town Saskatchewan.

In *The Glory Years*, Billy Harris tells the story of how Bert entered a summer shooting competition back home and ended up being charged with assault: "At rifle competitions, spectators could place money on who they thought would win, and if successful, they would profit. At [this] competition Olmstead had the lead, but on the final day he faltered and dropped out of first place. A gentleman who

Four key players on that first Stanley Cup team: Dick Duff, Tim Horton, George Armstrong, and Bob Pulford. At the Dearborn Inn, outside Detroit, Michigan, 1961.
BILLY HARRIS

had had a few too many cocktails came up to Bert in the men's room and accused him of 'not trying.' You could accuse Bert of a lot of things . . . but not of 'not trying.' Bert almost drowned the accuser by immersing his head in a toilet bowl."

If you look at the team photo from the 1961–62 championship team, the first thing that jumps out at you is all the hall-of-famers: Mahovlich, Kelly, Stanley, Armstrong, Horton, Bower, Pulford, Olmstead, Horton, Keon. But as Billy points out, the supporting cast was just as important. Baun, Brewer, Duff, Harris, and Ron Stewart would all score key goals in the Leafs' playoff runs over the next several years.

Most people think the last piece of that great Leaf team fell into place in 1960 when a diminutive, slick-skating 20-year-old named Dave Keon surprised everyone and made the team out of training camp. Keon started on a line between Dick Duff and George Armstrong — not bad company for a rookie — and won the Calder Trophy that year, ahead of teammate Bob Nevin.

Howell, Horton, Hadfield, Baun, and Prentice. At a party at a friend's house after a golf tournament.

BILLY HARRIS

P UNCH IMLACH PROVOKED the ire of his players more than once by saying that it was he who won that first Toronto Cup, but there's no denying he played an important role. In an article by George Gross of the *Telegram* from the late 1960s, Tim was asked, after all his time with the Leafs, to compare the coaches he'd played under. King Clancy was a strong motivator, and very close to his players. Howie Meeker was known for his backbreaking practices. Joe Primeau, Tim's favourite coach, was a quiet teacher of the game who rarely raised his voice. His nickname, even back when he was a player, was "Gentleman Joe."

"It was just the opposite with Punch," Tim told Gross. "If he had stopped screaming, we would have gone for the doctor."

Imlach was a bombastic, intense man who put results before friendships. As far as Punch was concerned, you were either with him or against him. If you were with him, Punch showed a lot of loyalty. If you were against him, it was almost impossible to get out of the doghouse. And Punch demanded a lot from his star players.

Johnny Bower remembers the typical dressing room scene, between periods after a Leaf goal-against:

"Punch would come in the dressing room and say, 'Horton, I told you a hundred thousand times' — that's what he'd always say, 'a hundred thousand times' — 'to make sure the players in front of you are not behind you.' Tim'd say, 'Sorry Punch, I thought he was there.' 'Well, he wasn't, 'cause he went by you and went on in and scored on Bower.' Then he'd go after me. 'And Bower what were you doin'?' And I'd say, 'Well, Punch, I guess I made the wrong move.' And he'd say: 'Yeah, you make a few more wrong moves like that you'll be back in the American League.' And I'd be thinking to myself, 'Oh no. Not again.'"

I never really said much to Punch in the Toronto years. I used to write him nasty letters from time to time about the way Tim was being treated — I was mad, for example, when Punch made Tim practise the day Traci was born. On another occasion, with four sick children at home, I had to handle the unpleasant task of having the dog put down when Imlach refused to allow Tim to skip an extra practice. Tim used to take me on road trips every now and again, and of course, Punch hated that. Someone asked him once what the perfect team was, and he said "a team of bachelors." But for some reason Imlach let Tim get away with murder. I remember a reporter once asking Punch whether Tim got excited before a game, and Punch replying, "Oh yeah. We have to wake him up to get him onto the ice."

Red Kelly tells me that he and Tim even snoozed through many of Punch's patented between-period pep talks:

"Tim and I sat next to each other and people would accuse us of sleeping. We worked hard on the ice and we knew what we had to do when we got back out, so we wanted to get our rest. And so Punch would be giving the pep talks and we'd played enough years to know what it was all about. We weren't really sleeping; we just had our eyes closed and got a good rest."

Years later, when Tim and I were in Buffalo, I'm not sure whether it was Punch who mellowed or me, but we got along great at that time. I never disliked the man, because Tim was so happy with the team when Punch was running it, but he was a real tyrant at times, and I didn't care for his methods.

TIM WAS A UNIQUE PERSON in a lot of ways. When you talk to his teammates now about the kind of guy Tim was, you'd think they were describing two different people. I didn't really run into Tim's wild side until after we had been married at least eight years and had all of our children. Over

Here's Tim in his Clark Kent glasses. ''Tim and I did a TV interview one time. They had this chalkboard there and the interviewer drew out a play and asked what we would do on this play. Tim started to answer him, and I guess I must have barged in and taken over, because afterwards Tim said: 'I'm not going to do an interview with you again. You wouldn't let me say anything.''' (Allan Stanley)

HOCKEY HALL OF FAME

the years some of the players let stories slip about some of his off-ice exploits — in the dressing room, at team parties, and on road trips. Sometimes I thought he was very funny and other times we would fight over his behavior. The girls all thought their father was funny, but I was far more in love with the Doctor Jekyll character, without a doubt. As the years went by the fights became worse. But even I had no idea about the extent of it until later years, after Tim was gone.

On an everyday basis Tim was a soft-spoken, likable, serious kind of man who shunned the limelight — very devoted and affectionate with his children, generous with friends and neighbors, slow to anger and quick with a smile. He was good with people and could talk to just about anyone and treat them like an equal. But he hated to stand up and talk in front of a crowd. When he was asked to speak at a banquet, he was nervous and uncomfortable and couldn't wait to sit back down.

Dave Keon still remembers this side of Tim most fondly: "He didn't really have any mood swings; he was very stable. You never really could tell whether he was up or down because he didn't show it. If he was down, he kept it inside and if he was up, he also kept that to himself. When it came to hockey he was always on an even keel, never got bent out of whack about anything. That was my impression of him. He'd been through some bad times with the Leafs but when I played with him there weren't many bad times and he took the good things in stride. He liked to have fun; he wanted everybody to be part of the fun and he made sure that everybody was involved."

For some reason Tim was particularly keen on getting Keon, Duff, and Mahovlich "involved," partly because they were young guys, and maybe partly because they'd all played junior at St. Mike's. "For some particular reason Duffy and I were called the 'singer midgets,'" Keon remembers, "and Tim felt that it was his responsibility to 'look out for us.'"

Frank Mahovlich says the young players soon knew that Tim had "a Jekyll and Hyde kind of personality":

"He was just not the same person after a few drinks. And the other players knew it and they would egg him on, encourage him. He'd do something crazy, and then the next day you'd wonder where the guy had gone — I mean where was that guy we were with last night? It was really strange."

This is from a party on Warden. Tim clowning around over Ron Stewart's shoulder next to a typically battle-scarred George Armstrong.

BILLY HARRIS

TIM BECAME INFAMOUS among his teammates for one stunt I didn't hear anything about until years later. On road trips the players were often given a curfew, usually 11 o'clock, by which time they were expected to be in their rooms, and hopefully, asleep. Tim didn't have much use for curfews, and when he'd come home late after a few too many beers, he apparently didn't have much use for anyone who did. Any teammate who wasn't up for a late night knock on the door was just as likely to see the door come down. When Tim was in one of these moods, other players on the team admit frankly to being scared of him.

"When Tim was tight I wasn't frightened for him, I was more frightened for myself. He scared the hell out of me," Armstrong admits, "and what he thought was fun sometimes spooked other people. He would never try to hurt anybody, nothing like that, but he was stronger than average and he didn't need any doors."

The players on that Leaf team were particularly fond of riding each other. Tim was picked on for being blind, Duff because he was religious, Mahovlich because he was "lazy,"

88

Stanley because he was slow, Keon for being small. From time to time Tim and Frank would really go at it, and when they did, Mahovlich would brace himself for a late-night visitor:

"Allan Stanley and Tim, of course, were always chummy and always together. One night Davey and I went out with them for a few drinks. We left them at the bar and went home, and with curfew, believe it or not, we were in bed where we were supposed to be. So Tim came home at about one o'clock and banged on the door, and I could hear Stanley egging him on. So Tim said, 'Open the door!,' and Davey started shouting 'No! No!' and Boom! The door came off. Honest to goodness a gorilla couldn't knock down that door. And yet Tim came right through. I looked at the screws and the hinges — you know it was almost inhuman the strength of the guy — and he just came right through it. And when the detectives came up, it ended up being me and Davey who had to pay the $100 fine and the expense of putting in a new door."

"I was on the inside a couple of times," Armstrong remembers. "One night we were at the Empress Hotel and Tim came down to see me, and Sammy [Stanley] was there with him as well. Allan was always in on it, and we heard him coming down the hall. Tim wouldn't do anything wrong or anything, it's just that if you were in bed he'd just take the bed over and to hell with us, you know. He'd just make a mess of your room and you didn't want to let him in. Anyway, this night I can hear him coming and I'm telling my roommate, 'Keep quiet, keep quiet, maybe he'll go by.' But of course somebody says, 'Hey, the Chief's in here, we gotta get the Chief.' So Tim knocks on the door and I wouldn't answer it. And Tim shouts 'I know you're in there, I know you're there you turkeys! I'm coming in.'"

"This was a solid oak door, about so thick, and I pushed from the inside, and he was hammering on the outside. And there's no question the door would have come in if I hadn't been on the inside pushing out. He did manage to crack it halfway across though. He finally gave up, and when I saw him the next day he says 'Where were you last night?' And I told him I was at home in Toronto. And I never told him I was in there."

After a few incidents like this, Tim developed a reputation as a door-crasher, and all it took was one pint too many

Horton Just Doesn't Get Mad In Play

Poor Vision Didn't Stop Horton From Developing Into First Class Player

By JIM PROUDFOOT

TORONTO, Ont.— At Maple Leaf Gardens the other day, the hot stove forum was debating the toughness of various National Hockey League players. Names like Gordie Howe, Lou Fontinato and Pierre Pilote were mentioned. Then Punch Imlach, coach and general manager of the Maple Leafs, took the floor.

"I think the strongest, toughest player in the National Hockey League is Tim Horton of the Leafs," he stated. "In a way, of course, you can't call him a really tough player because he's not mean the way, say, Howe is. Tim has to be riled up. But when he is, he's the best. I've seen enough movies of him in action to know that."

By no stretch of the imagination could Horton be classified as a rough or crude hockey player. He never has surpassed 94 minutes in any of his 10 NHL seasons and his yearly average is around 70 minutes, which works out to approximately one minor penalty every two games. That is practically Lady Byng deportment for an aggressive defenceman like Horton.

However, Horton's well-controlled Irish temper has been known to boil over and at times like that he utilizes tremendous physical strength. With muscles on top of muscles, he is about as powerful a player as there is in big-league hockey. Teammates think that in the service department of Tim Horton Motors, he holds the cars up when they are getting grease jobs. Tim can manhandle any player in the League and that includes strongmen like Bobby Hull and Jean Beliveau.

One memorable incident developed last winter when Horton, seated on the Leaf bench, was watching teammate Bert Olmstead absorbing punches from Lou Fontinato, then with New York Rangers. Tim finally couldn't stand it any longer, jumped over the boards and picked the 200-pound Fontinato bodily off Olmstead. Tim then started in to throw a few punches of his own. This touched off one of the liveliest brawls seen at

Musclman Of The Leafs

Tim Horton . . .

Brother Jerry Once Rated Good Prospect By Bruins

TORONTO, Ont. — Major league hockey almost had two Hortons. Tim's brother, Jerry, once was a highly rated prospect in Boston Bruins' organization and played for their farm teams in the Ontario Hockey Association's junior "A" series. He now plays senior hockey in North Bay.

the Gardens in recent years.

"I started it, all right," Horton admitted later, his normal good spirits having returned. "I'm getting a little old for that sort of thing."

In fact, Horton became 32 years old on January 12. That qualifies him for membership in the Toronto veterans' club. It is almost 13 years now since Myles Gilbert Horton graduated from Toronto's St. Michael's college and turned professional with Pittsburgh Hornets of the American League.

It took him three seasons of AHL apprenticeship before he earned promotion to Leafs in 1952. It was during his stay at Pittsburgh that he met his beautiful wife, Lori, a professional figure skater at that time.

The Horton career breaks down into three main sections. First, there was Horton the uninhibited, dashing rabble rouser who was on the NHL's second all-star team following the 1953-54 sea-

. . . He Started It

son. Then came a slight decline dating back to a 1955 accident when his jaw and leg were broken in a collision with Rangers' Bill Gadsby. Now you have the mature, skillful, disciplined Horton of last season and this, how come?

Well, Tim was plagued with a persistent, mysterious leg injury

Tim Not The (Of Hortons |

TORONTO, O ton probably is player with his wife, Lori, and daughters, do par work for a Toro

last winter and games because o failed to produc he decided to again.

"Rest isn't help as well be play Tim reasoned.

But a funny Since Horton cou his customary a unable to go on long charges do defensive work i had to improve his old status as top rearguards.

Horton's puck plus a booming s have made him a of Leafs' attack. made him a prin Toronto fans. H best rushing hockey and his of the hardest t scored 46 goals in NHL campaigns. fact, he even ha at right wing du regime as Leafs'

Horton has on of poor vision. I ing room, he is l or Cousin Weake he wore contac playing and ord the rest of the doesn't and his e a problem. Occas track of the puc enough to worry l

Jut-jawed Tim to the NHL in Leafs' last Stanle 1950-51 club. The ambition in 1 or five seasons-; win the world pri pionship. Seconda be recognition Leafs never have ciate his worth. been a regular, four years with Sam) Stanley.

Horton and Sta
(Continued (

GET TIM HORTON'S PICTURE FREE FROM BEE HIVE GOLDEN C(

Follow ple of — enj CORN bread, pancal

All th and C key pl recon HIVE (exclusi

For a free picture of Tim Horton or any member of Montreal Canadiens or Toronto Maple Leafs send one Bee Hive Corn Syrup collar or token; top from Durham Corn Starch or Ivory Laundry Starch; collar from St. Lawrence Corn Oil 25 oz. One collar, top, or token for each picture. Show your name and address, name of player you want, and mail to:

ST. LAWRENCE STARCH COMPANY L Dept. "H", Port Credit, Ont.

Mounted pictures measure 5" x 7"

The Start Of The Horton Family

When Tim Horton, right, was playing with the Pittsburgh Hornets of the American Hockey League in 1952 he met pretty wife, Lori, a professional figure skater. Frank Mathers, then a defenceman with the Hornets was best man at the wedding.

Article from *The Hockey News,* just before the Leafs' first Stanley Cup run.

A Tribute to Tim Horton

and the encouragement of a drinking buddy to get Tim going. After a few years of this, as Billy Harris reports in his book, the Leafs players got into the habit of leaving their doors open until they knew Tim was safely tucked away in bed. Nobody could tell me exactly how many hotel doors Tim had broken down over the years — but Armstrong guessed the total at about 60. Tim's teammates were sometimes stuck with the bill; in Pittsburgh, where Tim played late in his career, alternate captain Keith McCreary used to take up a collection from all the players to pay for the damage because they didn't want the coach (Red Kelly) finding out about it.

IN THE EARLY 1960s, teams still did most of their traveling by train, often catching an overnight trip after an evening game. There was a pecking order to the way the teams took berths on the trains — rookies got upper bunks, veterans, lower bunks. Back in Toronto players would have team parties, and particular friends on the team, but there weren't the same opportunities to bond as a group as there were on road trips.

"There's a great deal now made about a lack of male bonding [in the NHL] and how we need to get back to that kind of team feeling," Keon says. "When I turned pro we had our bond. We traveled a lot by train and did things together. As rookies you knew you were going to have to go through an initiation, you just didn't know when. It usually happened on a train trip back from Chicago. But when there were six teams there were always seven train trips from Chicago, so you didn't know which one it would be and you were always on pins and needles. Tim was the strongest guy on the team and he would always lead the initiations; he loved doing it. He'd let you know it was going to happen but he wouldn't tell you when."

Allan Stanley was another veteran Leaf who played a key part in terrorizing the rookies. He tells a story of one Horton-led initiation which took on a life of its own:

"We'd have a couple of beers on the train, get wound up, and we'd have to initiate the rookies. It usually involved a stripping, a shaving (and it could be a shaving anywhere), and sometimes a dyeing."

"Normally it's an initiation of the rookies, but it must have been a longer trip than usual, because this one time

91

they really got carried away: they were initiating everyone on the train."

"At that time, Foster Hewitt was also traveling in our car — he always got a lower berth at the end. When it came time, somebody said, 'Let's get Foster.' So Tim went into the berth, picked him up, and was carrying him up and down the aisle like a baby. After that bit of fun was over they decided not to initiate him after all and just put him back."

"They went on to do all of the players except two, and one of the things they liked was a guy that fights. They were going to get Dicky Duff, but no sir, he wasn't going down without a fight. He put up a hell of a battle. But Tim and Shacky got him right down, spread-eagled on the floor. Dick's stomach and chest was covered with thick black hair, and everybody knew that Dicky didn't know whether to get married or become a priest. So they shaved a cross on him, and of course he was upset. Then Tim said 'Well, let's get Shacky.'"

"So Tim is coming up the aisle, and Shacky is coming back towards him. Tim picks Eddie up and puts him on his back in about a second and a half, which is quite a feat in itself. Shacky is a very strong guy. So they initiate Shack."

"When that was over, of course, Shacky says, 'Let's get Tim.' Well, they had about ten guys, eventually, trying to get Tim down, and when they finally did it Dicky was right there, and he had Tim right by the you know, he was still mad [about the shaving], and he was squeezing, saying 'You son of a bitch, I'm gonna get you.'"

"So they got Tim. They did everyone except Bert Olmstead and me. I was in my berth by the time I heard Shacky say 'Let's get Sam.' But Tim says 'Nobody's touching Sam.' At this point I'm just bundled up in my berth like Foster, you know. Shack came for me, Tim grabbed a hold of him and they started wrestling. They had a hell of a fight but there were no punches thrown. But Tim wouldn't let them get me."

It's hard for people outside hockey to look at some of this behavior as "fun," but that's exactly how the people involved remember it. And one of the things you notice after hearing enough initiation stories is that the victims in one story are always the collaborators in the next. I've

Red Kelly, with his wife Andra in their living room in Toronto.

run into a lot of people in recent years, not just Tim's teammates, but guys like Ted Lindsay, Billy Harris, and Phil Goyette, and a lot of the fellows from the Montreal teams, and we often get to wondering whether the players on the ice these days are as close as the guys from those years *still* are. Players in this era make a lot more money and after a game they tend to go their separate ways — they really haven't built up the camaraderie they had in those days.

Tim used to ride his fellow players off the ice, in a good-natured way, but on the ice, he would not tolerate opposing players taking liberties with his teammates. Punch Imlach used to say Tim didn't have a mean bone in his body. It took a lot to get Tim angry, but when he did, no one, no matter what size, wanted any part of him. "Tim wasn't afraid of anybody," Dick Duff insists. Tim's nickname with his teammates in Toronto was always "Tiger."

Several of Tim's teammates recall a particular incident when Lou Fontinato jumped on Bert Olmstead's back during a game in the 1961–62 season. "Louie got out of the penalty box and he just pounced on Bert," Red Kelly remembers. "And our bench was on the other side of the ice, but Tim just flew out there and yanked Fontinato right out of the picture." Tim pulled Lou off Bert's back, threw him to the ice, then started pounding him. Tim used his fists very rarely during his career, but he was so angry over that particular incident he was ready to take on the whole

93

opposing team. Fontinato ended up in hospital. Tim would not tolerate anybody playing dirty with his teammates.

"He was my protector," Keon remembers. "Eddie Shack and I used to sit beside each other in the dressing room. When Shacky got traded he told me, 'I'm gonna get you.' Later we were playing against the Bruins; I turned away and Shacky saw it and he really hit me. Tim went right after him. And Tim was shaking Shacky around and Eddie was saying, 'He knows, he knows! I told him I was going to get him!'"

I T HAS BECOME A cliché these days to speak of someone as a 'team player,' but if the label ever fit anyone, it fit Tim. If you talk to any of Tim's old teammates, it's what they recall most about Tim as a player. Red Kelly, who not only played on four Cup winners with Tim in Toronto, but coached him when he was with the Penguins years later, perhaps puts it best:

"He was always with you or behind you. You just don't know how much that means to a team. What Tim did was never important to him, it was always what the team did, and *that* was what made Tim a great player. When I coached him it was the same way — he was the hub of the team. He was there, the strength supporting the club, and everybody felt 'Tim's back there. We're solid.' Nobody was going to be taking advantage of anybody on the ice, because Tim was there to support you. And he did."

A trip to Marine World, California, 1964. Left to right: George Armstrong, Carl Brewer, Dave Keon, Tim, and Ron Ellis.

BILLY HARRIS

94

One of the reasons Tim was able to play professionally for so many years was that he always kept himself in superb condition.

"He was the only guy at that time in hockey who focused on fitness," Eddie Shack remembers. "He was way ahead of his time that way — working the body, working with weights, developing the upper part of his body. He did push-ups and chin-ups. Just enough of everything to stay in good shape."

Tim, Bobby Baun, and Eddie Shack, chowing down at a pre-game meal in Long Beach, California, pre-season, 1964.
BILLY HARRIS

Tim had no particular love of practices; he told someone once that that he was "paid for practices"; the games he played for free. Still he was always one of his team's hardest workers. Well into his forties, when he could easily have asked his coaches for some leeway, Tim would take his regular turn in drills and scrimmages.

"He never, ever, took a night off," Keon remembers. "I don't think he knew how strong he was. And he was so determined. I used to say that if they were going to move the Gardens, Tim would get on one side and they could get a thousand people to move the other side. And he'd tell them don't worry, just make sure you don't drop your side."

"One night when I was playing against him, Timmy got his stick caught in my skate — this was years later when he was playing with the Rangers — and he thought I was holding his stick [with my hand] and he was skating off the ice and wouldn't let go. Tim had his back to me, and I was yelling at him to stop, I mean I was screaming at him, but he kept pulling at it. And he was so strong that when he turned and pulled on the stick he nearly tore the ligaments in my knee. Finally he saw me and let go, and said: 'Oh, I thought you were holding my stick.' To this day my ankle still hurts sometimes. I used to have to tape it because it was so badly sprained."

Johnny Bower remembers one afternoon when Tim tried to help him prepare his goal-sticks.

"After the team meeting was when everybody taped up their sticks, and one day I was in the little room and I had about six goal-sticks out. I always liked a goal-stick that was fairly light with a stiff shaft. So I was in there with Tim and Tim asks, 'Whadda ya doin'?'" I told him I was trying to fix my goal-sticks, and he says, 'Well, what's wrong with it?' I said, 'I don't know, I think this one here's too whippy for me — feels good, but it's too whippy. I like a stiff shaft.'"

"So Tim says, 'Well let me see it. I'll tell you whether it's stiff enough.' Well he took it out of my hands, put it down and snapped it right in half."

Tim at a Christmas Party, 1962. That's Bobby Baun under the Santa mask.

BILLY HARRIS

"'Yeah, it's too whippy!' he says. A brand new goal stick. I told him, 'It's a good thing Mr. Ballard or Smythe didn't come in here, or I'd be paying fifteen dollars.' He didn't know his own strength, for godsake. I could barely bend the thing."

W HEN A FELLOW IS that strong, his teammates have a tendency to test him when they get the chance. Tim's teammates are all fond of telling the story of a night in Quebec City after an exhibition game when the local authorities were required to shut down one of Tim's strongman routines. Every player, whether they were there or not, seems to have a slightly different version of the events of that night. Though the incident occurred after a night on the town, according to George Gross, there were only three people actually there — Tim, Bob Pulford, and Karl Ellief the team's physiotherapist. The three men were on their way back to the hotel after a few too many pints when Pulford spotted a construction site near one of the main thoroughfares. Bob and Karl challenged Tim to move one of the huge garbage cans filled with construction debris which were sitting by the road.

Red Kelly picks up the story:

"Pully was goading Tim and saying, 'You think you're strong. But you're not so strong. You couldn't even pick up one of those cans.' Of course that's all you needed to say to Tim to get it moved. And so he's picking them up — and they were full of cement — a normal person couldn't budge them, but Tim's sort of tossing them into the street."

Traffic began backing up on the street, the noise was tremendous, and it wasn't long before someone called the police.

"So *clangity clang!*, they go banging down the hill and the next thing you hear is the *clang clang* of the cop cars coming," Kelly continues. "The cops jump out and they want to get him into the car and he's got one hand on one side and one on the other, and there's three cops with their shoulders to him and they can't get him in the dang car. One of them takes a billyclub and bangs on his hand, and eventually they got him in there. So they took him down to the station and put him in jail."

Tim was charged with disturbing the peace, and they called Punch, who had a number of friends on the police

Tim at a party on Wedgewood, 1963.

BILLY HARRIS

97

force. Punch went down to the station, paid what he had to pay, and brought Tim back to the hotel. Tim was in his room with Allan Stanley a few hours later when he realized the police had failed to return his Stanley Cup watch. Ignoring Allan's pleas, Tim put in another call to Punch, this time to ask him if he'd please go back down to the station and retrieve it. Punch told Tim he'd get him another one, and to go to bed. Which is what Tim finally did, but not before he broke down Duffy's door to say goodnight (which Sam says Tim did every night). A bus arrived at 6:00 a.m. to take the team to the airport and a plane to their next game in Saskatoon.

The summer following his arrest, Tim returned with me to Quebec City for a holiday. One of the first things he did was write a postcard to Punch Imlach: "I've been here three hours and nothing's happened yet, but if it does, I'll call you."

Of course, this was an event that I, as Tim's wife, was definitely not supposed to know about. But when the *Globe and Mail* showed up the next day there was a small item on the front page saying Tim and Pully had been arrested the night before in Quebec City, and it also turned up as a news flash all day on the radio station I was listening to. The kids arrived home for lunch in tears because they heard their Daddy was in jail. Bobby Pulford was always a very quiet guy, so it wasn't too hard to figure out who was responsible.

I find it a funny story now, but at the time I was furious. Tim and I had had a long talk about his drinking and he'd promised to cool it on this road trip — a three-week

Christmas party, early '60s. That's me with Bert Olmstead, and Tim clowning around with my niece Willie. Although Tim would frequently wear those black glasses at home, after his injury with the Leafs, he stopped wearing anything for his eyesight on the ice. He got through the exam at training camp each fall by memorizing the eye chart.

exhibition tour in which Quebec City was the *first* stop.

I tried to reach Tim by phone later in the day, and instead got somebody (George Gross, it turns out) who said Tim wasn't taking any calls. At that point I lost it. George put King Clancy on the phone, and I told him off as well. When Clancy put Tim on I told him not to bother calling me again (he did call and speak to the girls) and, when he got back, not to bother coming home. When the team arrived back in Toronto, Tim stayed at the Royal York for a few days. As luck would have it one evening our daughter Kelly was one of several little girls in the Guard of Honour for the Governor General at an event there. Of course, I had to take her and accidentally ran into Tim. He came home with us that night and all was forgiven.

Tim returned to Quebec City, with me, the following summer, and his first move after we arrived at the Chateau

Announcing

Studebaker's Newest Dealer

TIM HORTON MOTORS
6267 YONGE ST. WILLOWDALE

"The new '62 Lark is a championship car. It's as stingy on gas as Johnny Bower is on goals, and can seat six big players in comfort. Yet the Lark moves like Dick Duff and Billy Harris – fast, sure. You've got a powerhouse under the hood and unbeatable performance to match. The Lark is a rugged competitor, the best in any league. I've coached my sales and service team to give you the best possible attention and satisfaction, so come on in and see us. Let my sales team arrange a test drive in the great new Lark for you."

FRED CARE and TIM HORTON
TIM HORTON MOTORS

HERE'S THE HIGH-FLYING STUDEBAKER CHAMPIONSHIP TEAM THAT CAN'T BE BEAT!

LARK 4 DOOR SEDAN

LARK 2 DOOR SEDAN

Here's "big car" comfort at "compact" prices. What form! Tasteful, fineline styling. Big, comfortable, family-size interior beats them all for roominess. The Lark can really manoeuvre, easily working its way out of heavy traffic—into tight parking spots. Power-packed for flashing breakaways, the Lark features your choice of 6 or V8 engines, ranging up to 225 h.p. Both engines are mighty easy on gas. The new Lark is rugged and it should be with its body-on-frame construction. All in all, the '62 Lark has all the performance and luxury features to put the competition on the seat of its pants.

NEW '62 LARK DAYTONA SEDAN

The pace-setting Daytona combines the high performance of a sports car, plus the luxuries and conveniences of a touring car—a combination that's hard to beat in any league! No other "sports sedan" in its class can match the eager Daytona. Wood-grain finish instrument panel, deep-pile carpets, spacious interior room. Available with standard, automatic, 4 speed floor shift and overdrive transmissions, your choice of 3 top-performance engines, luxurious bucket seats.

NEW '62 GRAN TURISMO HAWK

No other car offers so much to the discriminating motorist—prestige, performance, timeless design. Yet the exciting, boldly-styled Gran Turismo Hawk is priced at least $1,500 less than the competition! Drive the '62 Gran Turismo Hawk and experience its thrilling performance.

NEW '62 LARK STATION WAGON

You can seat six in solid, stretch-out comfort. Or add the optional rear facing seat, and you have comfortable seating for 8. Load the ample 72 cubic feet of space to the brim — the Lark is endurance-built to take it. The tailgate opening is a big 45" x 29¾". Test drive this, the handsomest, handiest and hardiest of all station wagons on the market.

TEST DRIVE *a new* **'62 LARK**
STUDEBAKER

YOU'RE A WINNER WITH LARK!

TIM HORTON MOTORS
6267 YONGE ST. — 222-2501

Advertisement for Tim Horton Motors, which Tim ran in partnership with Fred Care, on Yonge Street in Willowdale.

WILLOWDALE ENTERPRISE, DECEMBER, 1961

Frontenac was to write Punch a postcard: "I've been here three hours and nothing's happened yet, but if it does, I'll call you."

Then we walked around the city until he found an identical garbage can — he wanted to show me it was no ordinary garbage can. Life with Tim had its ups and downs, but it was never dull.

I N THE EARLY 1960s things were getting hectic in our home life. We'd had our last and youngest daughter, Traci, at that point, and we'd moved into a house on Wedgewood Drive in Willowdale. Tim worked in the summers until he got into business for himself, and then we'd never see him; he'd be working 16 hours a day. Shortly after we moved into Wedgewood, Tim and a friend, Fred Care, who had had a lot of experience in the car business, leased a BP station on Yonge Street just south of Steeles Avenue. It had a large lot which Tim and Fred stocked with cars. They sold Hillmans for Rootes Motors, and Studebakers. Tim spent so many hours at the lot, the girls and I would have to go there if we wanted to see him. Fortunately, the business was only a five-minute drive from the house. Even before then we used to see more of Tim during the season than we did during the summer. Except on game days, Tim would just go to practice and come home. Of course there were away games and the wild road life, but in the days of the six-team league traveling wasn't nearly as extensive as it is today.

The kids were all very close to Tim, but especially the oldest and youngest, Jeri and Traci, both classic Daddy's Girls. Before she started school each year, Jeri would run a fever and get very ill when Tim left for training camp. Her doctor said it was nothing but separation anxiety. Tim used to call Traci "Charlie," and she was with him all the time. He would take her with him to practice, the office, anywhere she wouldn't be a problem. Until the day he died Tim made a practice of checking each of the kids in their rooms and kissing them goodnight; on nights he came home late he would do it even before he removed his coat.

Traci had to have surgery at the age of five to correct a blockage in her intestines. The surgery lasted five-and-a-half hours, and because we were friends with a nurse in the recovery room she allowed Tim and I in to see her afterwards. Tim took one look at his little girl with tubes coming out of everywhere, still unconscious, and promptly passed out.

Tim would regularly bring teammates over to the house for dinner, especially the young single guys who didn't have families of their own yet. Bobby Baun and his (now ex-) wife Sally did some baby-sitting for us in those early years when he was still with the Marlies. Dicky Duff, who the girls dubbed "Daffy Duck," was a frequent visitor to the house, and always arrived in time to tuck them in. Later on, Bob and Margie Nevin watched them for three weeks when Tim and I went on a cruise. Another one of the girls' favourites was always Billy Harris, who they still call "Billy Bee."

Tim had always called me "Rosie" until the comic strip "Andy Capp" was introduced and some of the younger players who spent quite a bit of time at our home began calling us Andy and Florrie. I think Billy Harris was the chief culprit in this case, and while Andy didn't stick with Tim, his nicknames for me were always either "Florrie," "Flo," or worse, "Flossie the Flooze."

I used to go to almost all of the Leafs' home games. I had to have a very good excuse to miss one — only a sick child or a visit to the hospital would qualify. And even given my sometimes limited knowledge of hockey, Tim would always

Tim with Traci at the Santa Claus Parade, circa 1960. We used to go every year and watch the parade from a spot near the Gardens.

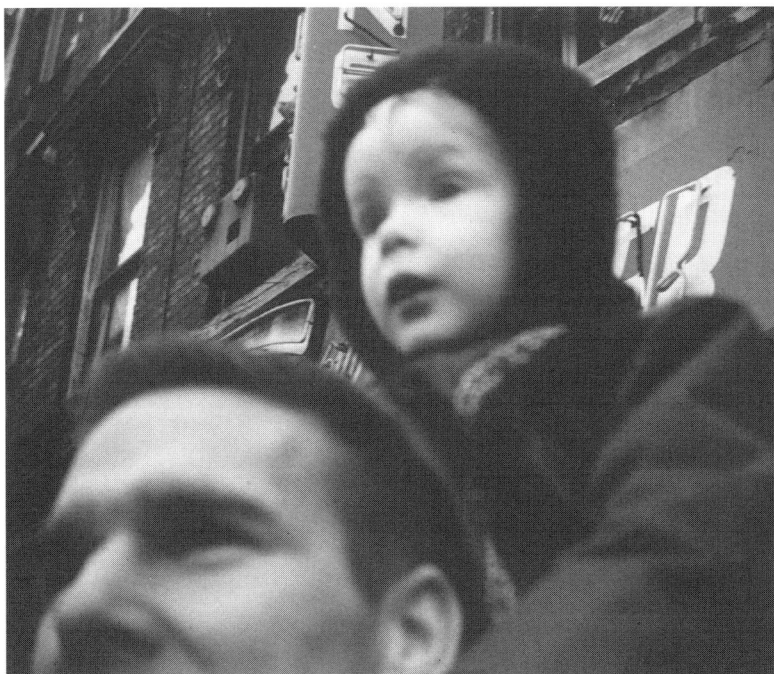

A daily occurrence in our house. The living room was seven steps up from the front hall, and when Tim came home, he'd barely be through the door before the kids would reach the top of the steps, and jump on him. And he'd always catch them.

FRANK LENNON

Tim and the girls at one of the annual Christmas skating parties. The kids loved the parties but hated the matching outfits I made for them. To this day they still give me a hard time about "dressing them funny."

HOCKEY HALL OF FAME

ask my opinion of how he'd played that night. I liked to disappear sometimes, so Tim finally got me seats in the Blues, right above the goal so there was no way he could miss me. If I got bored and read a book he'd catch me. If I disappeared with one of the other wives to the Hot Stove Lounge for a period, I would get told off after the game. Tim would come out on the ice before a game and he'd slap his stick on the ice, and the girls at home and I knew that was a signal from him that he was saying hi to us. He'd do that every game.

THE OTHER WIVES AND I would meet all the time, but the one day a year when everyone could meet each other's kids was the annual Christmas skate at the Gardens, which is a tradition that continues to this day. The kids would really look forward to the skating parties, but they hated the clothes I made for them — I would set them all up with matching outfits. But to this day they still give me a hard time about it — they insist I used to "dress them funny." Frank Mahovlich remembers them always looking cute, and for years the family picture appeared on the front page of the *Globe and Mail* sports section. But they hated me for it.

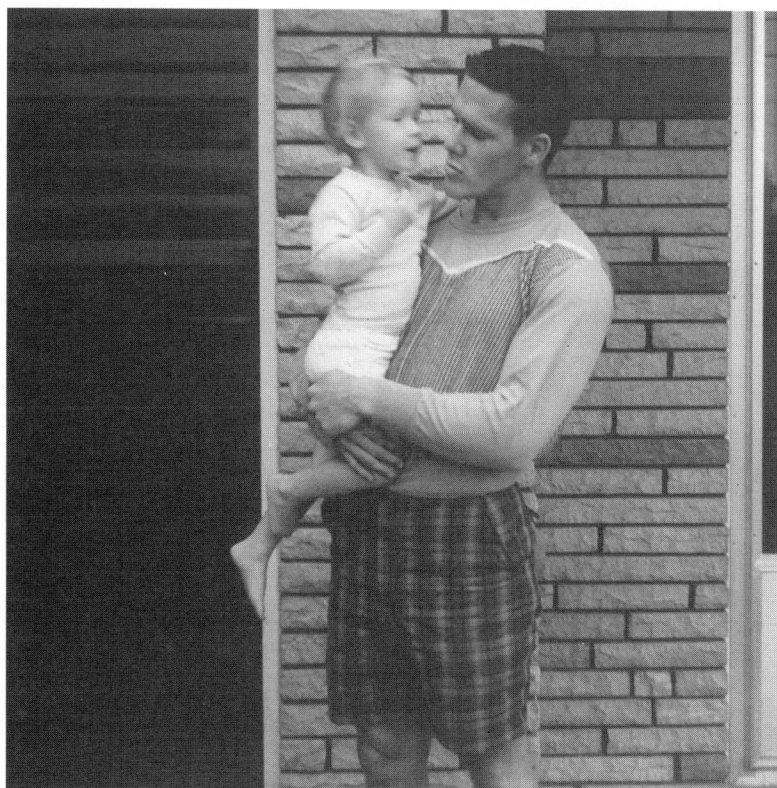

Kelly, putting on her holster, Christmas, 1960. All my kids were tomboys. None of them had any interest in dolls or anything girlie, but the cowboy gear went over well.

Tim (with Traci) dressed in some awful plaid shorts. Tim was always a real sharp dresser — anything he picked up, he put on.

105

Have the good time of your life at the Canadian National Exhibition ... Pan-Am Games ...

Creative Pantino/Panteen.   **STETSON**

At one point or another, everyone in the family did some modeling, and in this ad even Tim got into the act. But he never really dressed well until Michael Stern started making clothes for him. When Tim showed up for the fitting, they couldn't believe how he was dressed. That's Kelly with the camera and me in the funky paisley number.

Tim himself was a confirmed slob. He didn't care what he was wearing; anything he picked up, he'd put on. The kids were sometimes embarrassed to go shopping with him. He used to wear a favourite shirt until it fell off him. Late in his career, after he left the Rangers and went to training camp with Pittsburgh, a group of his old teammates from N.Y. came and presented him with a Superman T-shirt. Tim wore that until it was in shreds; at one point he had to put a safety pin in the shoulder or it would have fallen off him.

At one time most of the Leaf players ordered their suits from a place called Tony the Tailor in Montreal. Tony usually did a pretty good job, the suits looked nice and the price was reasonable. The Leafs had a dress code back then, even though nobody was making a lot of money. But there was one top coat that Tony made for Tim that was so big he could have used it for a tent. Tim took a lot of abuse from the guys over this coat but he still wore it for years. I even went out once and bought him two new top coats, but Tim lost the first game he played after wearing one of them, pronounced it "unlucky," and returned to wearing the old one.

Then one year, Tim, Kim, Kelly, and I were asked to do a photo shoot for one of the newspaper's weekend magazine and Tim was sent to a men's wear manufacturer — Michael Sterns — in Toronto. The people there couldn't believe the way he was dressed when he arrived for a fitting, and they decided they would dress him from then on. From time to time Tim would come in and select a fabric and they would make him the suits. I would choose the shirts, ties,

THE TELEGRAM, Toronto, Sat. April 17, 1965 83

Dick Loek, Telegram

Eight-year-old Kelly Horton may be the daughter of a well known Toronto Maple Leaf hockey player and she is already a fashion model with a mind of her own — but to be seen in a Montreal Canadien sweater. Well!

Kelly modeled at the CNE fashion show several times. The organizers knew Tim would be in the audience watching, so they sent her down the runway wearing a Montreal Canadiens sweater. As you can see, Kelly enjoyed ribbing her dad.

TELEGRAM PHOTO

Four all-time Maple Leaf greats (left to right): Armstrong, Horton, Keon, Stanley. They're all in the Hall of Fame, as are about a half dozen of their teammates from the early 1960s.

and socks, and for the first time Tim started to dress well.

Tim got his first new clothes just in time for a Stanley Cup party at Stafford Smythe's house, and Eddie Shack promptly threw Tim and his new suit into the pool. Stafford loaned Tim one of his — several sizes too small — and Tim wore that for the rest of the evening.

Though the clothes did change, it took the girls and I forever to convince Tim to let his hair grow, but he finally agreed. I think he got better looking as he got older. Apparently, I wasn't the only one. In 1974, Tim got a kick out of an article in the *Toronto Star* fashion section which had him mentioned — with the likes of Robert Redford, Yul Brynner, Telly Savalas, and Burt Reynolds — as one of the "Sexiest men in the world." When he was told about it, Tim immediately got himself an extra copy, walked into Punch's office, and plopped it down on the boss's desk. "And you thought you were only paying me to play hockey!" Tim said.

Kim inherited Tim's strength. Though she's slim and very feminine, her physical strength is quite amazing. When she was about eight months old, I had her in her playpen

Tim with Allan Stanley after the 1961–62 Cup. It was perhaps the best few weeks of hockey Tim ever played. He led his team in playoff scoring that year, an accomplishment for a defenseman in any era, let alone the early '60s. His 16 points (3 goals, 13 assists) at the time was an NHL record for playoff scoring by a defenseman.
IMPERIAL OIL LIMITED, TUROFSKY COLLECTION, HOCKEY HALL OF FAME

outside my kitchen window and when I checked her she was heading down the driveway with Punchy going crazy alongside her. She had removed two spokes from the play-pen to make her escape.

Kelly was a quiet, happy, dainty little girl who was over-shadowed by Kim when they were kids. Kim would make all the requests and demands for both of them, and Kelly would just chime in with a "me too."

All of the girls modeled with me at one time or another, and one year at a CNE fashion show Tim was in the audi-ence, so the organizers sent Kelly down the runway wearing a Montreal Canadiens sweater. Kelly had a great time teasing her dad.

TIM'S BEST PERIOD AS a hockey player may have come during that first Stanley Cup run in 1961–62. Tim started playing very well just before Christmas and carried his play right through the playoffs into the finals. He led the team in playoff scoring that year — something almost unheard of for a defenseman, and his 16 playoff points (three goals and

13 assists) at that time set an NHL record for playoff scoring by a defenseman.

There were a lot of hockey people, including legendary hockey boss Jack Adams, who saw Tim as the league's best defenseman that year. Then, as now, votes for league trophies were conducted after the regular season. Maybe things would have turned out differently had the voters been able to watch Tim's playoff exploits, but Doug Harvey won the Norris Trophy again that season, and Tim didn't even make it as a second-team All-Star. For some reason Tim never had much luck with individual honours, despite the high esteem in which he was always held by hockey people. He was voted an All-Star six times in his career, but he never won the Norris Trophy, finishing runner-up twice: to Pierre Pilote, and later, Bobby Orr.

The 1962 Stanley Cup parade. That's the Toronto crowd on Queen Street near the cenotaph at (the old) City Hall. The team came down Yonge Street in cars, but the players had to get out and walk through Simpsons to get to City Hall.

I T'S VERY DIFFICULT to describe what it was like to win that first Stanley Cup. Toronto hasn't won now in 30 years, so a lot of people aren't old enough to remember it. I think we had a party every night for three weeks afterwards; it was bedlam really, but an awful lot of fun. The Leafs clinched the win in Chicago that first year, so I wasn't at the game, but we were all at the airport to meet them coming in. Tim had been in Toronto 11 years at that point, so the first one was incredibly exciting. The people turned out *en masse* for the parade the next day. I remember I was standing up by the cenotaph near City Hall — the old City Hall — and I remember

hearing a woman near me, very excited, saying "Look! I've got a piece of Allan Stanley's hair." It was craziness. The players had to get out of their cars and walk through Simpsons department store to get to City Hall; the cars just couldn't make it through the crowd anymore. We were all up front for the ceremony, but the crowd was so big the police had to hold them back to protect us.

The next year, after a second Stanley Cup, we took a plane to Florida and were on the same flight as Stafford Smythe and Harold Ballard, who were heading to their homes in Del Ray Beach. Tim and I were on our way to visit my sister and her husband in Hollywood, Florida, but we got together with Staff and Harold for an evening out. After dinner and coffee they all started telling dirty jokes (my sister included). The jokes got so bad they all had their napkins over their faces, and I had to leave the table. I don't consider myself a prude, but these jokes were *bad*. We went to a dance club later where my sister and Stafford entered a twisting contest and tried to bribe the MC into letting

The crowd was so large for the City Hall ceremony that the Leaf wives and families had a police escort. The girls and I are somewhere up in front to the left of the policeman in the centre of the picture.

**Tim with Red Kelly
and Tim's long-time
friend and St. Mike's
teacher, Father
Flanagan, at one
of the parties.**
IMPERIAL OIL LIMITED,
TUROFSKY COLLECTION,
HOCKEY HALL OF FAME

**Tim, me, and our photogenic daughters at City Hall
after the 1964 cup. I did not make these outfits for my
daughters, which may explain why they are smiling.**
GRAPHIC ARTISTS/HOCKEY HALL OF FAME

The 1962 Cup parade. I remember hearing a woman near me, very excited, saying, "Look! I've got a piece of Allan Stanley's hair!" It was craziness.

them win. The bribe was not accepted, but they took second prize anyway.

Tim and his mates would win four Cups in total with the Maple Leafs in the 1960s — three in a row in '62, '63, and '64, and another "surprise" win three years later in 1967.

Tim was never one to be in the middle of the fray during the post-Cup celebrations. He tended to hang back by himself and look on, excited, but kind of taking it all in. He rarely joined the celebratory antics, except when it

Tim with Tim Daly during the '62 parade. Daly had retired in 1960, but was the trainer on seven Stanley Cup winners during his tenure with the Leafs, dating back to 1932.

TORONTO MAPLE LEAFS
STANLEY CUP CHAMPIONS — 1961-62

FRONT ROW — LEFT TO RIGHT: *Bert Olmstead; George "Punch" Imlach, Manager and Coach; Ron Stewart; Mr. Conn Smythe, Chairman of the Board; George Armstrong, Captain; Stafford Smythe, President; Tim Horton; Harold Ballard, Exec. Vice-President; Allan Stanley; Frank "King" Clancy, Asst. Manager and Coach; Dick Duff.*
CENTRE ROW — LEFT TO RIGHT: *Bob Haggert, Trainer; Carl Brewer; Bill Harris; Bob Nevin; Johnny Bower; Bob Pulford; Bob Baun; Don Simmons; Tom Nayler, Asst. Trainer.*
BACK ROW — LEFT TO RIGHT: *Dave Keon; Larry Hillman; Leonard "Red" Kelly; Frank Mahovlich; Eddie Litzenberger; Al Arbour; Eddie Shack; John MacMillan.*

The 1961–62 Stanley Cup champion Toronto Maple Leafs, one of the best hockey teams ever assembled.

came to throwing Punch into the shower (fully clothed, of course). After the Leafs won their third Cup in the spring of 1964, Punch had been through enough of these post-game dunkings that he'd deliberately brought a second suit. The problem was, he'd forgotten to bring extra shoes. I remember at the post-game party, which was held at a restaurant on Bloor Street owned by a friend of some of the players, Punch walked in with bare feet. Bare feet but a dry suit.

Politically, the Cold War was in full force, and it would still be several years before something like the 1972 Canada-Russia series would even be considered, but in the winter of 1965 a top Russian team visited Canada to get a first-hand look at NHL hockey. One of their stops was Maple Leaf Gardens, where they were particularly impressed with the play of a certain defenseman, Tim "Hortonov."

"He is a formidable defender," one player told Maple Leaf Gardens' P.R. man Stan Obodiac through a translator. "He plays guard very well. He plays hard, but cleanly. . . . He is a very good skater and his whirlwind rushes up the ice are very pleasing. His shot is powerful when he is in

114

IN RUSSIA, THEY'D CALL TIM:

HORTONOV

Master of Sport

By STAN OBODIAC

TIM HORTON
His play impressed the Russians.

WHEN the Russians were here to watch NHL hockey, they were asked which defenseman impressed them the most.

"Number 7," they said, "Hortonov."

Elaborating further, they gave their reasons: "He is a formidable defender, he plays guard very well; he plays hard, but cleanly — you never see him giving an elbow into the teeth, which we find not good about NHL hockey; he is a very good skater and his whirlwind rushes up the ice are very pleasing; his shot is very powerful once he is in the enemy zone. In our country he could very easily have the title, Master of Sport."

When Horton was told, by way of an interpreter and by way of an admiring intermediary, that the Russians considered him the best defenseman this side of the Volga, that he was a defender they had not even seen in

HORTON likes his food, owns doughnut firm.

28

the days of Stalingrad, that he skated like a sputnik taking off for Mars, the big, stocky Tim just grinned and said: "Very flattering in a way. Maybe they will put me on the negotiation list of the Bolshoi Ballet."

* * *

Horton is one of the humorists with the Leafs and usually his habit is to answer with some wit, burst into. a grin, settle down and then talk seriously. Right now when he grins you notice the stitches in his forehead.

"There are 17 or 18," says Tim. "I had the wound twice. First, Sam (Allan Stanley) shot the puck and hit me, and it was just getting healed when Gordie Howe whacked me again."

Last year Horton finally made an NHL All-Star defense berth, an honour too long denied him. So far this season not too many have been talking about him repeating.

He says: "I certainly have not been as productive early this term as I was last. Which makes a big difference. The All-Star selectors usually go through the goals and assists columns to decide; they overlook many other important aspects of the game. Then once they have made their mid-season choices they stick with them at the end of the season, no matter how good a second half a fellow has.

"I seem to be doing everything about as well as I did last year. But I personally don't know whether I'm playing better. I only try to play as well as possible; others assess me. But the points will come. When you get points, they come in clusters. A scoring burst often is only confidence at its highest during such a run. Last year I got a great many points in the first

half. Guys were tipping in pucks for me. This year it hasn't happened as much."

The cluster may now begin for Horton as last Saturday he scored a goal just after Carl Brewer did — the rarity of two defensemen scoring goals back to back. It was his second goal of the year. The goal seemed like a shot of adrenalin into the area wherever confidence lies in the body.

Of course the Russians aren't the only ones to recognize the ability of Tim Horton.

* * *

Eddie Shore, one of the greatest defensemen in the history of the NHL, once said that the 5' 10" 185-pound Horton would be one of the three best all-time blueline defenders in the league.

"He has the proper skating technique," said Shore, who reveres this aspect of hockey, "which enables him to get the most out of himself with the least effort. He puts the work on his thigh muscles when he's skating and he keeps his head up."

Conn Smythe, a pretty good evaluator of hockey talent too, noticed Horton when he first came up from Pittsburgh and termed him "the best defense prospect in Canada."

Horton has teamed with Allan Stanley for a considerable length of time. "For a brief spell I played with Kent Douglas but Sam and I have been a pair for six or seven years. Even off the ice we spend a lot of time together. He is one of the best defensemen, has been for a number of years."

Stanley occasionally does some rushing, but Tim has been acknowledged one of the best rushing de-

Continued on page 48

According to Gardens PR man Stan Obodiac, when a top Russian club team came through Toronto in the winter of 1965, they were particularly impressed with a certain Leaf defender they called "Tim Hortonov." Seven years later, Tim was invited to try out for the 1972 Summit Series against Russia, but he declined, for a number of reasons.

MAPLE LEAF GARDENS

---

the enemy zone. In our country he could very easily have the title, Master of Sport."

On the way to Montreal for the first playoff game one season, Punch passed out a copy of Norman Vincent Peale's *The Power of Positive Thinking*. The book had a huge impact on Tim. He became an avid fan, attending Marble Collegiate Church in New York whenever he was in town and having transcripts of Peale's sermons sent to the house. It was only in the past five years that I began to understand what had inspired Tim so many years ago.

I MET SOME OF OUR best friends during those Leaf years through modeling. One day a group of us were sitting in the Blues at Maple Leaf Gardens shooting a commercial and

Larry Mann, Canadian comedian and actor, who we met while shooting a commercial at the Gardens in the mid-1960s. Larry, Gloria, and their four sons were among our best Toronto friends before they moved to L.A. After that, Tim would visit the Manns every time the team was in L.A., and I joined him during a few of Tim's West Coast road trips.

a loud, booming voice called out "Lori Horton!" from ice level. I looked down and saw this person looking at me and said, "Yes?" He said, "You have four daughters!" and I said "yes" again, and he replied, "Well, we have four sons!" By this time I had recognized the fellow as Larry Mann, a well-known Canadian actor and broadcaster. What I didn't know was the extent of his whole family's hockey fanaticism. We saw a lot of each other over the next few years. My daughters used to go visit the Mann boys to play. At one point I found out the boys were putting Traci in the net as goaltender and shooting at her. At the time, Tim and I were not amused, but it became the subject of much laughter in later years. The Manns were great friends to a lot of the players, and a lot of us loved them dearly, including me and my daughters. When they left Toronto and moved out to L.A., I missed them terribly. Gloria Mann is a fountain of wisdom — very warm and generous — and the whole family has a sense of humour that never stops. My sister said one time after dinner at the Manns that it would be a wonderful house to lose weight in; they kept you laughing so hard during dinner you couldn't eat your food. Tim would visit the Manns every time the team visited L.A. and I joined him during a few of the Leafs' west coast road trips.

"Tim was one of the first guys I met who had a real family image," Larry told me recently. "I remember once when you and the kids came out to L.A. The kids were all playing in the pool, and just as we got around to them there was this tremendous crash out front. I said, 'What the hell is that?' and when I went out I found that Tim had parked the car — he wasn't used to the fact that we lived on a mountain — and he didn't leave the brake on. The car had careened down the street and hit a rock, which made it turn and go up backwards on my neighbour's lawn. And the fact that it hit that rock probably saved some lives. I remember you were giving Tim hell about leaving the brakes off, and I said, 'Hey, the man just saved I don't know how many lives! He should be congratulated!'"

Larry still shakes his head remembering Tim's strength, on and off the ice. For example, he remembers the night Moose Vasco — a huge man who played for the Blackhawks in the 1960s — made the mistake of grabbing Tim during a rush with Dave Keon into the Chicago zone. Tim dished the puck off to Davey, and in the time it took him to move in, score, and turn around, Tim had won the argument and was sitting on top of Vasco's chest saying "don't ever do that again." He also recalls a practical joke Tim played when we were all over at Larry's brother-in-law Harold's place:

"Tim needed somebody's phone number, and he said, 'Harold have you got a phone book?' We were in the den, and Harold told him to use the phone in the kitchen, where Tim looked up the number, called it, and then came back into the den with the telephone book and ripped it in half [lengthwise]. He handed it to Harold and told him, 'Here, you can keep this half in the den and the other half in the kitchen.' I'd never seen anyone do that before.'" Tim got such a kick out of it, in fact, that it became one of his regular tricks. For years, wherever we were, at home or away, no phone book was safe.

The Manns' oldest son, Danny, lived with us for a few months one year, and together we put on a party for Larry and Gloria's 25th wedding anniversary. The couple just celebrated their 50th in September 1996. And they've remained great hockey fanatics — their first grandson attended his first hockey game at the age of three months. I miss them and love them all very much.

Flanking Tim are Sid Queripel (left) and Roger Pelletier, who were Tim's closest friends outside of hockey. Roger died five years before Tim in an accident at work. His wife Renette is still one of my closest friends. We all met through our kids, really, who had modeled together.

My daughter Kelly modeled at the annual fashion show at the CNE for a few years. It was there I met two lovely ladies whose children were also in the show — Kathy Queripel and Renette Pelletier. The three of us became close friends and, to everyone's surprise, when our husbands (Tim, Sid Queripel, and Roger Pelletier) got together they found they really liked each other as well. The memories of our times together and the fun we had would fill a book, but Renette's friendship in particular allowed me to spend more time alone with Tim than I ever could have without her. Renette thought nothing of looking after the kids while I went on a road trip, giving me a freedom which didn't exist for other hockey wives with children. I still thank her for it, and we remain very close to this day.

Another person very dear to Tim and me was Bobby Baun's mother, Ethel, a very classy lady. Ethel and I went

These photos were taken at top of the Empire State Building on a New York trip after one of our Stanley Cups. That's me and Tim, and Allan and Barbara Stanley (below).

to out-of-town playoff games together and Tim visited her often because he loved her home-made biscuits. Tim referred to Ethel as "the old witch" because she was very adept at reading cards. The stuff she would come up with often turned out to be surprisingly accurate. She always told me I would marry twice, but would never divulge what was going to happen to Tim. Both Ethel and Bert Olmstead's wife Nora helped me out on separate occasions when Tim was out of town and I was too ill to clean the house. In recent years I've really noticed how most of the people I met through hockey were really wonderful people.

ONE WINTER, AFTER I'd returned home following a two-week stay in the hospital, I developed a lengthy and debilitating staph infection. The infection was serious enough that my doctor recommended that we go south immediately following the hockey season in order to heal my throat. When I got back, I could have my tonsils removed. While I was seriously ill the doctor would arrive at the house in a red MG wearing a red cap with matching scarf and gloves. The hospital wouldn't readmit me at that point, so he made daily house calls to see how I was. He was one of the few truly dedicated doctors I've met over the years.

Tim with my brother-in-law Danny O'Toole at his place in Holly-wood, Florida. Tim and Danny were two clowns on these trips; they took turns placing prank calls to each other from a nearby phone booth.

Somewhere along the way Tim had run into a lawyer by the name of Ken Gariepy. Though I have no recollection of when and how we met him, it feels like we always knew Ken. Tim and Ken became close friends and Ken became Tim's legal counsel for all of his personal and business affairs.

Tim and I followed the doctor's suggestion and booked a 21-day cruise with Ken and his wife Joyce, with stops in four ports in the Caribbean, through the Panama Canal, and on down the west coast of South America. The ship carried only 100 passengers, a small and intimate group who soon became friends. The ship also carried cargo, so we picked up coffee in Columbia, bananas in Ecuador, and shrimp in Buenaventura, Columbia. Tim's jacket (containing his only pair of glasses) went missing after our first stop in San Juan, Puerto Rico. Tim told everyone he'd packed only two pairs of pants to wear with the jacket, so he was in bad shape.

In Ecuador, bananas were loaded from barges on a river, up a ramp, and into the hold. The men were running up and down the ramp with huge bunches on their shoulders weighing 85–100 pounds each. It wasn't two hours before Tim decided to join them. At the end of the day Tim mentioned to one of the officers that these loaders had to be in great shape. He replied, 'Yes, but they only live to 40.' In Buenaventura, Tim befriended the crew of a Spanish

The great Jean Beliveau, chasing Tim behind
the Leafs' net. Stanley Cup finals, 1967.
GRAPHIC ARTISTS/HOCKEY HALL OF FAME

Bruins' Gilles Marotte chases Leaf Mike Walton while Stanley, Horton, and Johnny Bower watch the play unfold. DENNIS MILES

Tim and teammate Murray Oliver have their men (Wayne Connelly, and Garry Unger, respectively) in a thwarted try on the Leafs' net, 1968–69 season. The goalie is Bruce Gamble. DENNIS MILES

Eluding the always-dangerous Stan Mikita. That's Gamble between the pipes for Toronto. DENNIS MILES

Tim gets help from Stanley and teammate Brian Conacher (#22) in breaking up a Canadiens' chance on goal. Canadiens' great Yvan Cournoyer is in the crease. DENNIS MILES

Barry Cullen,
Murray Oliver,
Eddie Shack,
Ed Litzenberger,
and Tim have
a beer at Herb
Kearney's house
after a charity
softball
tournament,
circa 1963.
BILLY HARRIS

Tim and Bobby Baun
on a pre-season tour to
Long Beach, California,
September, 1963.
BILLY HARRIS

The whole family at City Hall,
after the 1964 Stanley Cup win.
GRAPHIC ARTISTS/HOCKEY HALL OF FAME

Tim with Phil Esposito, in Phil's office, in front of the opposition goal; I wonder how many goals Espo scored in exactly this manner. DENNIS MILES

The toothless wonders: Billy Harris, Tim, and Bob Nevin celebrate in the dressing room after the their first Stanley Cup win, 1963. BILLY HARRIS

Tim asleep up at the Griggs' cottage, mid-1960s. Tim could nap at a moment's notice. AUTHORS' COLLECTION

Tim on the ice with his old friend Bob Nevin, this time as New York Rangers; spring, 1970. DENNIS MILES

Tim playing against some of his old Toronto teammates, during his one season with the Penguins. Rick Kehoe is being covered by Tim in front of Pens' goalie Jim Rutherford.
DENNIS MILES

Pete Mahovlich, Frank's younger brother, chases Tim behind the Sabres' net during Tim's last year with Buffalo. Hard to believe they called Pete ``Little M.''
FRANK PRAZAK/HOCKEY HALL OF FAME

Tim's last game (against the Leafs), February 21st, 1974. The swelling on Tim's right cheek is painfully obvious.
DENNIS MILES

cargo vessel, and we finished the night on their ship (with Tim doing some "bull fighting") while our captain had the police out looking for us.

We got home happy (if a little overweight) and I had my tonsillectomy. The day I got out of hospital, Tim packed up the kids and headed off to North Bay. Our bedroom had a door leading out to backyard and the inside door was open. I was still too sore to sleep, so I was lying in the bed reading when, suddenly, Punchy flew to the door with his ears down, growling and barking. When I looked up I saw a man in a white shirt standing there looking at me. He was startled by the dog, and stood there long enough for me to get a good look at him. Then he took off. I called the police, who came and took a report, then called Tim who hopped in his car and came down to pick up Punchy and me and take me up to North Bay.

Though he never said so, I got the impression Tim didn't really believe me. My Peeping Tom returned a few more times when Tim wasn't around, but one night Tim practically knocked the man over going out through the screen door. The prowler took off running with Tim in hot pursuit. But Tim was going out into the dark from the light, he wasn't wearing his glasses, and he ended up running straight into a tree. Tim called the police and really blasted them for letting this go on so long. But that was the last we saw of our Peeping Tom.

Tim on a European vacation we took together. This is a lookout at the top of a mountain in the Alps in Switzerland. We were the only ones there, except for one other guy, and by coincidence, he knew Tim.

AFTER ABOUT FIVE YEARS of living on Wedgewood Drive we decided we should start looking for something a little larger. We had enough room for us and the kids, but when our families would visit from out-of-town we found ourselves cramped any time anyone came to visit. We looked unsuccessfully for quite a while. One day Tim was out of town and I was driving around and saw a lot for sale. I don't know where I found the nerve but I called the agent and bought it. Tim wouldn't even look at it for a while, but eventually he decided something should be done with it.

Tim had a friend, Ed Siekierko, a business partner and developer who built homes and small industrial buildings. Ed took a look at the lot and suggested that Tim build the house himself. Ed offered to help out with the sub-contractors, the architect, and personal advice and support.

Tim and the girls in a promotional photo from the mid-1960s.
That's Kim in the trunk, Jeri with the hand warmer,
and Kelly giving her father a happy look.

The plans were drawn up by us, permits were issued, and Tim went to work that summer. It was a ravine lot, near Leslie Street and York Mills in Toronto; there were woods and a little creek running through. Unfortunately, though, we hadn't had an engineer look at the lot and when we began digging the foundation we found the lot was on landfill. It took a solid week of trucks carrying away fill non-stop before he reached the proper depth to pour the foundation. I don't think a combination of earthquake, tornado, and hurricane could knock that house down.

I felt terrible. In one week we were already over-budget. Tempers flared and the stress level was very high. I stayed up nights trying to fit another bathroom into the plans. Tim would often stay at the house site having a beer or three at the end of the day with the workers, and we began fighting non-stop. My doctor recommended a psychiatrist for me; I agreed and made an appointment.

One night we had dinner at Roger and Renette Pelletier's house. It was about two in the morning and Tim had had quite a bit to drink but he insisted on driving. I wouldn't get into the car with him, so he took off and left me to walk home. I'm not sure how far it was but it was a long way in the dark and I was terrified. Not too far from home a police car picked me up and drove me the rest of the way. It was after four o'clock when I got home and I went to bed and started crying. I was still crying when Tim got home a few hours later (he had stopped at Sally and Bobby Baun's, woke them up, and scared Sally half to death). When I hadn't stopped crying by the next afternoon, Tim called up the psychiatrist. He couldn't see me but he sent out a prescription anyway and told me to start taking the pills right away. At this point I hadn't even met the man. The pills were called Dexamyl and I was to take two tablets, three times a day. This was the beginning of a nightmare for me, though it would be years before I realized it. Dexamyl was a commonly prescribed drug at the time — I knew a few people who had taken them, and I had even had a few myself years before, so I didn't think anything of it at the time. I don't think any ill effects showed up for three or four years, but I might not be the best judge of that. I wasn't aware of the side effects later, even while I was having them.

Breaking ground for the house we built on Bannatyne Avenue in Toronto. I bought the lot on my own, without Tim ever seeing it, when Tim was away on a road trip. The trouble was, once we started digging, we found our nice ravine lot was sitting on landfill. It took a solid week for the trucks to haul all the fill away.

It took three months to get the basic structure of the house up, but we had to move in before it was finished because the kids had to start school. More specifically, the bottom two floors and the kitchen weren't finished. We barbecued and cooked what we had to in the rec room; it was a lot like camping out. The house, a corner lot at 105 Bannatyne Avenue, was finished before Tim went to training camp in 1964. I started decorating and life went back to normal. A few years later, we installed a pool in the back yard and we got a lot of pleasure from that with weekend pool parties, mostly with the Queripels and the Pelletiers. Our new neighbours, Bill and Audrey Landon, had allowed us to use their phone, water, and electricity while the house was being finished, and they fed us more than once over that first little while. When we got the pool, Tim repaid Audrey's kindness by picking her up (she was all dressed up and on her way to a wedding) carrying her from next door and dropping her into the pool. Audrey was such a good sport about it — she couldn't stop laughing.

In May 1965, Tim and I participated in a Sportsmen Show in St. John's, Newfoundland, and there was a dinner held there in his honour. I don't know if Tim was the first prominent hockey player who had ever visited St. John's, but I can tell you we were treated like royalty the whole time. The airport was just loaded when we arrived and cars followed us wherever we went. He was interviewed on every radio and TV station. A dozen roses would arrive for me at the hotel every morning we were there. We both were treated incredibly well and had a fantastic time. The only small problem we had was the weather — the fog prevented us from seeing as much of the scenery as we would have liked. I keep promising myself I'll go back, but I haven't yet. The people out there are just great people.

TIM HORTON DINNER
(Sponsored by Prince of Wales Arena)

The program for a dinner held in Tim's honour by the Sportsmen in St. John's after the 1965 season. Tim and I both loved Newfoundland, especially the people, who treated us like royalty.

IN CONJUNCTION WITH SPORTSMEN SHOW
MAY 18, 19 20

May 17, 1965 — 7 p.m.
Memorial University
Dining Hall

Autograph

Tim skating in the
All-Star game, 1964.
Tim had been named
a second-team All-Star
in 1953–54, but this
was his first, first-
team selection.

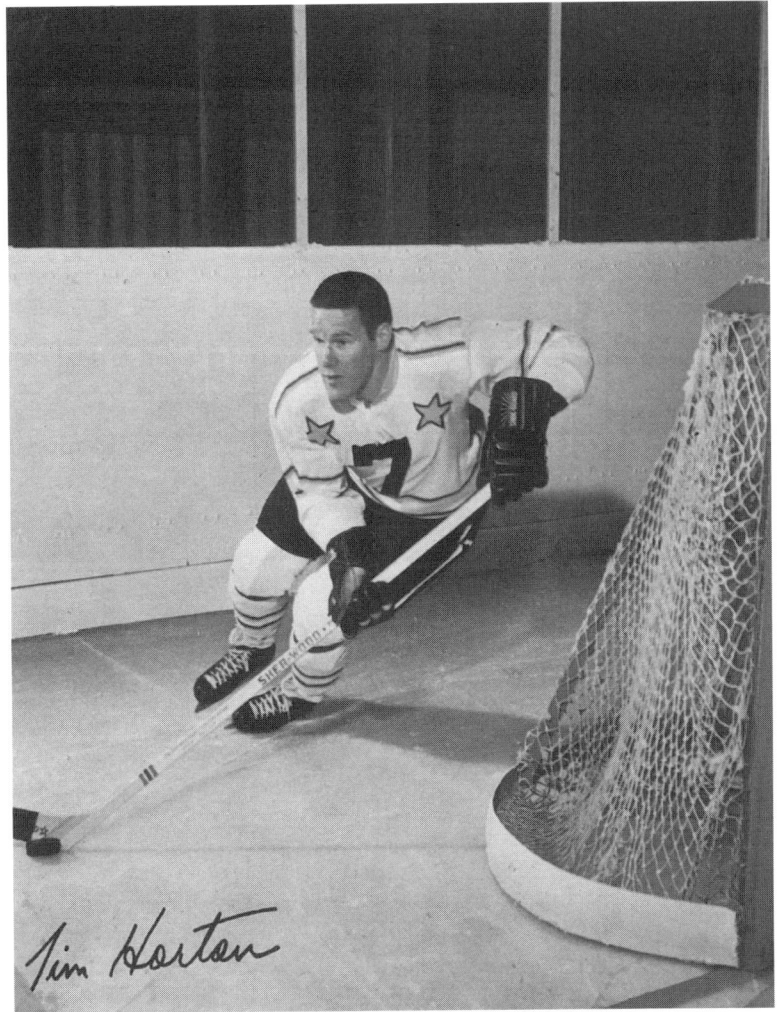

Tim Horton

IN TORONTO, THE PLACE the players got together in those
years was George's Spaghetti House, on Dundas Street.
"We always went to the same place — George's," Allan
Stanley remembers. "We used to go down there after practice
for lunch, as they called it. A lot of times that meant a liquid
lunch."

According to Allan there were a few groups among the
players. One group usually sat playing poker. Another
group, the group which included Tim and Allan, liked to
talk hockey: "After a few beers we straightened out a lot of
guys, you know. [Someone would say], 'You think you're
playing good hockey?' and away we'd go."

Dicky Duff remembers that one common argument had
to do with the forwards backchecking, and the Leaf team's
general emphasis on defense. Mahovlich, Keon, and Duff
whose job it was to score goals, used to argue that by
requiring the forwards to come back and help the defense,

the Leaf's style of play was costing the scorers a lot of points.

"Sometimes we would have a team discussion and I would go over this stuff with Tim," Duff remembers. "I said Davey, me, and Mahovlich should get 60 goals a year, but a guy who's backchecking is lucky to get 20. 'I mean if we're going to play this kiddy kind of hockey,' I told him, 'you guys will cost me 10–15 goals year.' So one night we were arguing back and forth, in a joking sort of way, and Tim and Allan opened the window on the second floor."

"Dicky was a yappy guy this night," Sam recalls, "he kept yapping and yapping and giving Tim hell. Tim of course just sat there taking it and I looked over at Tim and I said 'Are you going to take that from this little . . . ?' And I convinced Tim to go over and grab him, and he took him over to the window and hung him by one leg right over Dundas Street."

"They both grabbed me by one leg," Duff recalls. "They dangled me out the window, saying: 'How do you feel about the defensive team now, Dicky?' I kept quiet, and when they let me back in I ran for the door." True to form, once Duffy was safely outside, he started yapping again.

Evenings at George's were an important part of Leaf life, and they gave the players a place to bond off the ice. But the routine could also be hard on a player's family. I remember I didn't particularly like it; Tim seemed to be gone all the time. The odd time Tim would call me and invite me down for dinner, but there was more than one day when a players' "lunch" would last until three in the morning, and of course Tim and Sam were always among the diehards. But there's no question it played a big part in making those Leaf teams Stanley Cup winners.

Tim ties up Parker Macdonald of the Detroit Red Wings, circa 1964.

THE LEAFS' LAST CUP in 1967 was probably the least expected. A number of players from the early 1960s — Duff, Harris, Olmstead, and Nevin — had moved on to other teams or retired. And many of the Leafs' key players — Kelly, Sawchuk, Bower, Stanley — were either at, or pushing, 40 (Sam was 41). The team was up and down at the beginning of the season, and in January and February the Leafs went on a ten-game losing streak. The papers were on the players' backs, and things just seemed to go from bad to worse.

One night during the losing streak the team was leaving for Montreal late in the evening, and the Queripels and the

Three "Timmys," Easter Seal Calendar, 1965.

Pelletiers were over for dinner. We had a few bottles of wine; Tim had to leave after dinner, and he appeared in the living room wearing one of my wigs, a hat, and a foot-wide pair of sunglasses, carrying a box of tissues under his arm. I couldn't believe what he was doing, but off he went, dressed like that. At Union Station he ran into Sam, took his arm, and entered the station. As they passed through the gate and boarded the train, the television cameras were on, and after another loss that night in Montreal they showed the tape on the news and suggested Tim should have saved his disguise for *after* the game.

Punch worked the team harder over the next week but nothing seemed to go their way. When the Leafs slipped to fifth place, the pressure finally got to the Leafs' coach and Punch was checked into hospital for two weeks suffering from exhaustion. During his absence, King Clancy took over behind the bench and for whatever reason the team started winning again. The Leafs squeaked into the playoffs in fourth place, and no one gave them much of a chance in the semi-finals against the first place Blackhawks, where

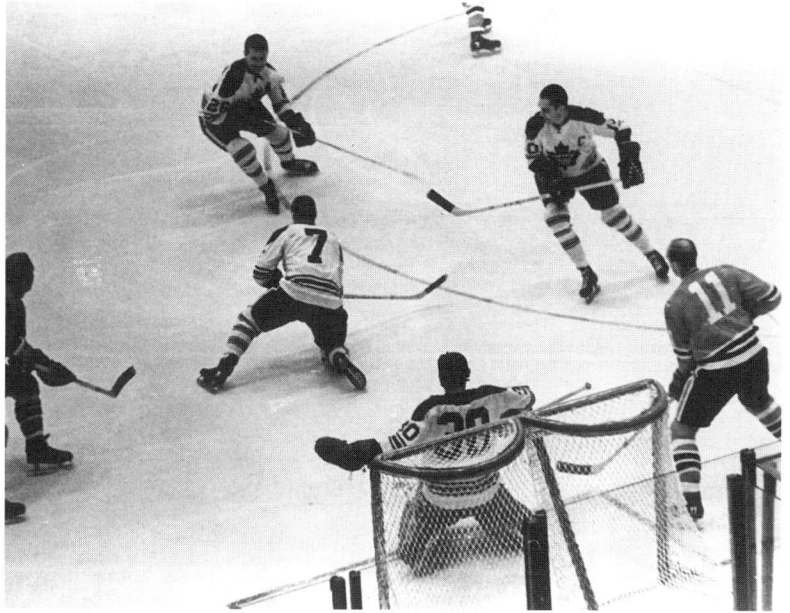

Tim blocking a shot in a game against the Hawks. Captain Armstrong is back-checking as usual, and Sawchuck is between the pipes.
HOCKEY HALL OF FAME

Mikita and Hull were in their prime. The Leafs lost the first game in Chicago, but with a determined, tenacious defensive game (and unbelievable goaltending from Sawchuk and Bower) they won four out of the next five, clinching the series at the Gardens in the sixth game. Both Sawchuk and Bower were injured during those playoffs but their great play continued into the finals against the powerhouse Canadiens.

Starting up ice from behind the net. That's Bower in goal, and Tim is sporting even more battle scars than usual.
IMPERIAL OIL LIMITED,
TUROFSKY COLLECTION,
HOCKEY HALL OF FAME

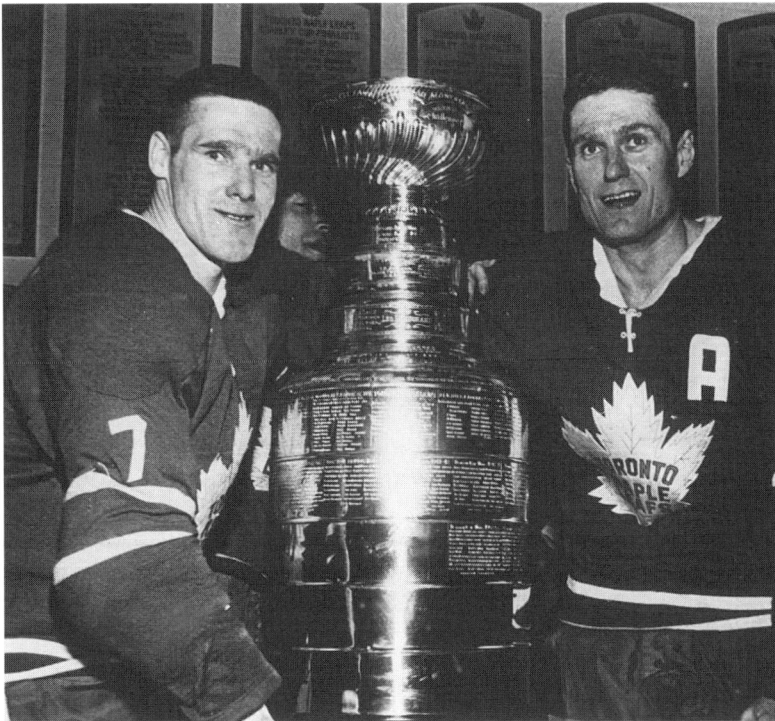

Tim and Sam with the "surprise" 1967 Cup, a win made all the more sweet because the Leafs were not expected to get by Chicago in the playoffs, let alone defeat the powerhouse Canadiens. "They had goal scorers, they had speed. If we let them in our zone, we were going to lose the series. . . . I think we played the whole series at centre ice." (Allan Stanley)
GRAPHIC ARTISTS/ HOCKEY HALL OF FAME

According to Allan Stanley the Leafs' game plan was simple: "It's not often that you get every single player on a team be absolutely honest with himself and say, 'This is what we have to do to win.' We had a team meeting before Chicago and asked ourselves how we were going to win this thing. The consensus opinion was whoever was on the ice, whoever was closest to Mikita and Hull, go stand next to them, don't let them carry the puck. Let them give it to anybody else; let the other guys try to beat you."

"And then against Montreal, Davey Keon was the one who came up with the plan. They had a powerhouse; they had goal scorers, they had speed. If we let them in our zone, we were going to lose the series. The only way was to keep them out of our end, which meant the defense had to stand up on the blue line and we had to have two guys coming back to cover the wings. That's how we played. I think we played the whole series at centre ice. We weren't a scoring team; I think we had about six guys on the team around 20 goals, but we were a good bumping team, we would take the man out of the play. And we had to play textbook hockey."

In the third game against the Canadiens, we had 28 minutes and 26 seconds of overtime before Bobby Pulford scored the winner. That seemed to be the turning point,

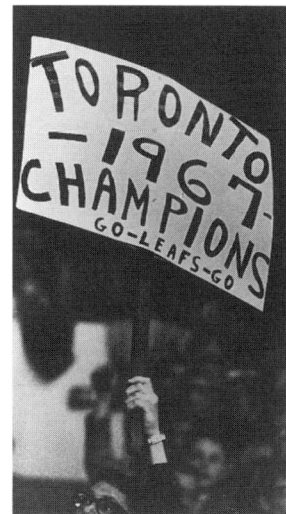

A Leaf booster during the 1967 Cup run.

TORONTO MAPLE LEAFS

1966-67

STANLEY CUP

AND

WORLD CHAMPIONS

Front row, left to right — "Punch" Imlach, manager-coach; George Armstrong, captain; John Bassett, board chairman; C. Stafford Smythe, president; Harold E. Ballard, exec. vice-pres; Bob Pulford; "King" Clancy, asst. mgr coach. Second row — Johnny Bower, Dave Keon, Larry Hillman, Red Kelly, Frank Mahovlich, Tim Horton, Bob Baun, Terry Sawchuk. Third row — Ron Ellis, Marcel Pronovost, Pete Stemkowski, Allan Stanley, Eddie Shack, Larry Jeffrey, Mike Walton. Back row — Bob Haggert, trainer; Milan Marcetta, Brian Conacher, Jim Pappin, Aut Erickson, Tom Nayler, asst. trainer.

Most Leaf fans think of the 1967 Cup as the end of a dynasty and the beginning of 30 plus years of futility. I remember it as the year Tim and his mates won a championship through sheer determination. Of course, having Sawchuk and Bower in net didn't hurt.

and the Leafs wrapped up the championship in the sixth game on home ice. In many ways that 1967 Cup was the most fun because it was so unexpected and seemed to have been won on sheer determination. As soon as school was out, our whole family went west to Las Vegas and the Grand Canyon, then out to California to Disneyland and a visit with the Manns in L.A. Larry even took us to work with him one day when he was doing a part on *The Man From U.N.C.L.E.* It was really a memorable trip for all of us.

Tim's one major individual honour (outside of All-Star selections) came when he won the Bickell Cup with the Leafs in 1969. The Bickell was something special if you were a Maple Leaf — it was not something they would give out every year, it is "awarded, at the discretion of the board of directors, to a Leaf for a tremendous feat, one season of spectacular play, or remarkable service over a number of years." Tim had had a spectacular season on defense; he was also considering retirement at that point and I think the Leafs wanted to honour him for all his years of service. Bobby Baun won the award in 1971 after a career in which he'd played so courageously in the playoffs, scoring that famous overtime goal in 1964 on a broken leg to force a seventh game against the Red Wings. When a person wins

Tim and the girls at the Grand Canyon, summer 1967.

John Bassett (and the great Foster Hewitt, not pictured) present Tim with the Bickell Cup, given to a Leaf "for a tremendous feat, one season of spectacular play, or remarkable service over a number of years." Although he was proud to be named, it also created a sore spot, as Tim was traded that spring and the Leafs, despite his repeated queries, never gave him the replica trophy to which he was entitled.

MAPLE LEAF GARDENS

133

That's me with Hugh Phillips, outside his house, summer 1997. Hugh's determination to overcome his cerebral palsy and live an independent life inspired Tim from the day he met him.

a trophy like that, he's given a smaller version of the real trophy to take home with him. But even these little trophies can be very valuable — the Bickell was solid gold and would have been worth about $10,000.

Tim was at a ceremony where Foster Hewitt and John Bassett handed him the big trophy, but he was never given his own replica. Tim was traded to the Rangers at the end of that year, and every so often Tim would ask about it, and they would always tell him it was down in the safe and they couldn't open it, or some such excuse. Tim asked about it every time he came into town; I even went down there once to get it, but they could never locate it. Off and on for years, Tim would complain that he'd won only one award in all those years with the Leafs, and they still wouldn't give it to him.

I N ADDITION TO HIS work as a player, Tim used to drop in at a hospital on Jarvis Street just south of Bloor in Toronto that used to be called the "Home for Incurables." I always thought that was an awful name, and was happy when they eventually changed it to "Bloorview." The hospital still exists but it has been moved up into North York. Tim dropped in after practice one day and stood and watched a young man around 11 or 12 years old who was disabled with cerebral palsy. He had on a pair of skates and was trying very hard to use them. He'd fall and get up, fall and get up, over and over and over again. Tim stood and watched him for a long time, amazed at the boy's determination. He just wouldn't quit; he didn't know the meaning of the word. And Tim told me later: "I've never seen anybody with guts like that."

Later he found out the kid had built the rink himself; he was that determined that he was going to skate. Of course he never did, but he didn't stop trying until they had to fuse his ankles and he just couldn't get his skates on anymore. His name was Hugh Phillips, and he and Tim became instant buddies. Hugh would visit us with his friend, Barry McMullen. We took him to hockey games and Hugh even joined the team in the first Stanley Cup parade and at the party afterwards, which he still describes as "the best day of [his] life."

This picture was taken by a fan who recognized Tim at a gas station, on our down way to Pittsburgh for a family visit. He was nice enough to send us a copy.

Hugh's courage, pleasant personality, and positive attitude, despite his disability, inpired Tim his whole career. And Tim's friendship, interest, and his own positive attitude inspired Hugh. Hugh honestly believes that despite his disability there's nothing he can't do, and he's proved it over the years. He's had a job since he was old enough to work, owns his own house, drives his own car, and until recently (when all his equipment was stolen), ran a successful landscaping business.

I'm so proud of Hugh; he's done so well for himself. Hugh and I get together occasionally and play "what if?" wondering how things would be different if Tim were still with us. Tim added so much to so many lives. Still we both know we were lucky to have him for the time we did, and there's nothing we could change even if we wanted to. Hugh still has trouble talking about Tim without breaking down.

On the way to the dressing room, during Tim's last year in Buffalo. That's Larry Hillman, the Sabres' other veteran defenseman, behind Tim.

BOB SHAVER

IV

"Horty"

I thought I was fine. I went to the game and it was funny; standing there for the national anthem, there was a minute of silence and it was like I felt everyone else's loss all at once, how the whole community felt about Tim and, Christ, suddenly there I was, crying to start the game. When I came to the bench, I was saying "I'm fine, I'm fine." But, of course, I wasn't.

— *Jim Schoenfeld*

TIM WAS THE KIND of person who didn't like to be idle. He always worked between seasons at some job or another to help the family get ahead, and for most of his playing days he was preparing, in one way or another, for life after hockey, which was only sensible given the relatively short careers most hockey players had, and how little they were paid. Tim had tried a few businesses of his own in the early 1960s with varying success. He and his brother Gerry ran a hamburger restaurant up in North Bay for a while. Later he had a gas station/car dealership on Yonge Street in Toronto. But playing hockey, Tim couldn't really devote enough time to either of these operations for most of the year, and as a result they were not successful in the long run.

For years and years on our trips down to visit the family in Pittsburgh there was a little donut shop in Erie, Pennsylvania, which Tim liked so much he would go well out of his way just to stop there. So he was a confirmed donut fanatic from way back. Still, given all of that, he really fell into the donut business by accident. We had an old friend,

The filing papers on one of the first two Tim Horton Donut stores, on Lawrence Avenue in Scarborough, franchised by Dennis Griggs. Griggs eventually sold his interest in the donut chain to Tim and his new partner, Ron Joyce.

DENNIS GRIGGS

```
           DECLARATION OF BUSINESS

COUNTY OF YORK    )
                  )
                  )
        To Wit:   )
                     4 TWEED CRES.
    I, DENNIS GRIGGS, of the Township of Scarborough, in the County of
York,


HEREBY CERTIFY

1.               That I have carried on and intend to carry
on trade and business as doughnut shops at 2016 Lawrence Avenue
East, in the Township of Scarborough, in the County of York, under
the name of "Tim Horton Donuts"
2.               That the business has subsisted since the
1st day of February, 1964.
3.               That I am the sole proprietor of the said
business.
4.               That I am of the full age of 21 years.



WITNESS my hand at Toronto,
this 18th day of February,
1964.
```

Dennis Griggs, one of the first people we met when we moved to Toronto. He had gotten involved in two donut shops, one on Lawrence Avenue near Warden and one on Avenue Road. The Avenue Road store eventually went out of business, but the one on Lawrence Avenue did quite well for a while. Dennis had introduced Tim to Jim Charade, from whom Dennis had purchased the place on Lawrence Avenue. Together they formed a company called Jimantim Ltd.

Jimantim opened a drive-in restaurant chain with three shops located in Scarborough, in Port Credit, and on Yonge Street, downtown. In 1964, Dennis, Tim, and Jim formed a new company called Tim Donut Ltd., licensing Tim's name for use in what they planned to be a chain of donut shops. The first Tim Horton Donuts was opened in Hamilton on Ottawa Street. Dennis had acquired all the equipment for the store and had also signed up the first franchisee — a man named Spencer Brown. The store did very well from the start; in those days donuts went for 69 cents a dozen, and a cup of coffee cost a quarter.

But the drive-in restaurants, despite doing what seemed like a lot of business, were still losing money. Tim and I came home from a South American trip one day to discover the restaurants were completely out of money and the chain close to bankruptcy. By this time a second donut shop had been opened in Hamilton. Because of the success of the Hamilton shops all three partners knew the business had potential. But both Dennis and Jim Charade ran into financial snarls: "It was just a matter of not enough working capital," Dennis remembers, "getting too big, too fast. My stores went down first, I signed them over to Jim and Tim, and at the same time I signed over my one-third share of the company. Then all three went down, and Jimmy signed his shares over to Tim."

Ron Joyce, a former Hamilton police officer and Tim's future partner in Tim Horton Donuts was not, as is commonly believed, one of the company's founders. Tim met Joyce after Jim and Dennis had pulled out, when Ron franchised the first and second donut shops, both in Hamilton. The first had had two franchisees before Ron took

TIM DONUT LTD.
(OPERATING TIM HORTON DONUTS)

TIM HORTON
PRESIDENT

874 SINCLAIR ROAD
OAKVILLE, ONTARIO
TELEPHONE 845-6511

Tim's business card for Tim Donut Limited, which he and Ron Joyce operated out of an office in Oakville.

The "Big Seven" restaurant Tim opened with his brother up in North Bay. Above the doorway was a drawing of Tim playing hockey, and his signature.

The first box design for Tim Horton Donuts. The logo is closer to Tim's actual signature, and featured four donuts, one for each of his daughters.

WE USE ONLY 100%
PURE VEGETABLE OIL

Tim driving his favorite car, a Sunbeam Tiger. It was a little British sports car with a big engine, and a lot of fun to drive.

over. In the meantime, Tim, Ken Gariepy, and myself were the officers of the company and Tim ran the business from an office at home. Ron bought my 50% of the shares in the company in 1967, and they gradually built up the business until there were more than 30 stores by 1972.

From the beginning the business plan was sound; the only real obstacle the partners faced was gathering enough working capital to get each franchise up and running. The store sign and trademark box featured Tim's signature (as it still does) and an oval depicting a stack of four donuts (one for each of his daughters).

MANY OF TIM'S TEAMMATES from the early 1960s were gone before that last Leaf championship in 1967. Olmstead retired after the first Cup. Dick Duff and Bob Nevin went to the Rangers in the Andy Bathgate/Don McKenney trade, Billy Harris had gone to Detroit as part of the Marcel Pronovost deal, and Carl Brewer retired in 1965 after a blow-up with Punch Imlach. Over the next two years, the dismantling of the team continued. Bobby Baun and Terry Sawchuk were lost in the 1967 expansion draft, Frank Mahovlich was traded (with Garry Unger and Pete Stemkowski) to Detroit for Norm Ullman and Paul Henderson in March, 1968. In fact, by this time the players from the Leafs' Stanley Cup teams were spread so widely around the league, Billy Harris says the ex-teammates had a running joke going about it. Players would call up their ex-mates, collect, from all parts of the continent, often in the middle of the night. The goal, aside from waking each other up, was to keep the other guy talking — on his dime of course — for as long as possible.

After bowing out to the Bruins in four straight games in the 1969 playoffs, Imlach himself was fired in April, despite the fact he had just guided the Leafs to their 11th straight winning season. By that time, Tim and Ron Joyce had reached 12 franchises in their increasingly successful donut operation, and Tim found it harder and harder to meet the demands of player and businessman. Tim would be 40 that January, and with George Armstrong and Johnny Bower both retiring at the end of 1969, he had all but decided to join them.

Stafford Smythe and Harold Ballard were temporarily removed from the daily operations of the hockey team while they dealt with tax problems, and in the meantime the team was run by a group of executives in their absence.

In the early days of the business, deals were settled with a handshake, and Tim kept most of his information in this little black pocket daytimer. Note the franchise fee ($5,000) and start-up capital ($2,000) estimates.

**Tim started Tim Horton Donuts at that
desk, which is still in my daughter's house.
That's Traci being teased by her father.**

With the Leafs primarily a team of youngsters — with
Pulford, Ellis, and Dave Keon the only key players left over
from the championship teams — the Toronto brass was
anxious to have Tim back to bring along some of the team's
young defensemen. As a joke as much as anything, Tim said
he'd return happily — at twice his current salary (which
was about $40,000 at the time). Tim was as surprised as

**I don't know if Dini
Petty will ever speak to
me again for putting
this photo in. It's her
first wedding (she was
still in her teens), and
the marriage didn't
last very long. Kelly
was Dini's flower girl
and I sang at the
wedding. We met
through her mother,
who was an agent
for commercials.**

Star photo of Tim and Traci during his first "holdout" in the fall of 1969. The Leafs had to double Tim's salary (to $80,000) to prevent him from retiring. Tim worked on one-year contracts for the remainder of his career.
DOUG GRIFFIN, TORONTO STAR

—Star photo by Doug Griffin

HOMEWORK TAKES PRECEDENCE over hockey with Tim Horton. Leaf's all-star defenceman, holding firm to decision to retire from game, sits at home helping daughter, Tracy, 9, with her schoolwork while club flounders through exhibition schedule. Only money — in large quantities — could alter his status.

Horton continues to hold firm

Tim met Tiny Tim the night he went down to sign his last contract with the leafs. Tiny Tim was a big Maple Leafs fan. They seem like an odd couple, but the two Tims got along great.

Tim looks on as his mates cover up in front of the Leafs' net in a game against the Rangers from the late 1960s. The goalie is Bower and Ron Ellis is in the crease with him.
GRAPHIC ARTISTS/HOCKEY HALL OF FAME

143

Picnic with Allan
Stanley at the Beehive,
a place Allan owned
at one time in
Bobcageon, in Ontario
cottage country.
To my eye, Allan has
barely changed since
those years.

Publicity photo from when Tim worked
promoting construction safety during
his years with the Leafs.

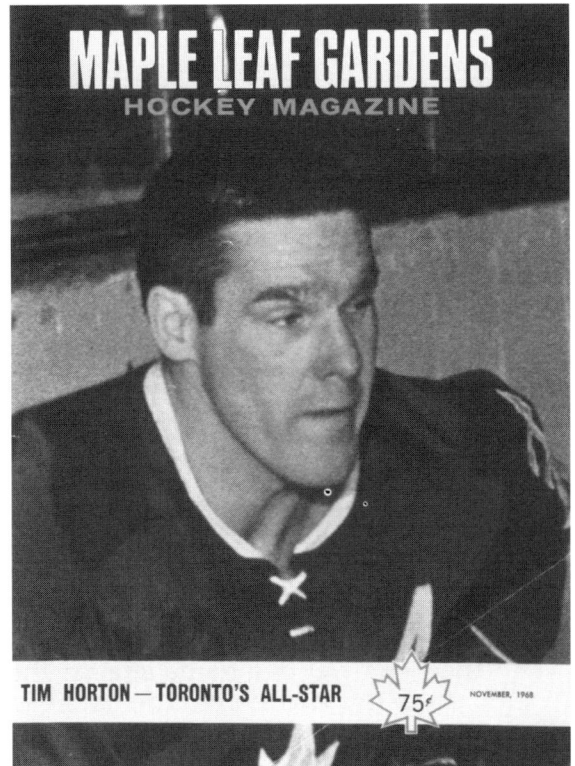

MAPLE LEAF GARDENS
HOCKEY MAGAZINE

TIM HORTON—TORONTO'S ALL-STAR 75¢ NOVEMBER, 1968

Leafs' program, 1968.

Tim with trainer Bobby Haggert. Allan Stanley and I were at the Hall of Fame recently looking at a bench he thinks is from the Leafs' dressing room. Tim hated sharp skates, so he used to rub them on the bench after he'd had them sharpened. The bench at the Hall of Fame has marks on it just like the ones Tim made. But there's no way to be sure it's the same bench.

anyone when, about two weeks into training camp for the 1969–70 season, the Leaf management agreed.

This would be the first of five consecutive one-year contracts for Tim, who contemplated retirement every spring only to be lured back for one more year at the end of the summer. But it would be his last campaign as a Maple Leaf.

Toward the end of the 1969–70 season it became clear to the Leafs that they were not going to make the playoffs. Tim was still playing near the top of his game, and at least two teams approached Toronto about Tim's availability. St. Louis was interested, as were the New York Rangers, who were Cup contenders that year, but had lost star defensemen Brad Park and Jim Neilson to injury.

The Leafs gave Tim a choice as to where he wanted to go.

Tim standing next to Bobby Orr on the East Division All-Star team, 1968–69. Bobby told me once that as a kid he patterned his game after Tim's.

Retirement was again in the back of Tim's mind, but another pay hike was involved (this time to $100,000) and the thought of another chance at a Stanley Cup had a certain appeal. After discussing it with me and the kids, Tim agreed to go to the Rangers in March of 1970.

"I would have turned it down had my wife Lori, and my daughters had any objections," Tim told George Gross in a *Telegram* article after the trade. "They come first. I talked to my wife . . . and I called my children at home. They all encouraged me to make the move." Toronto eventually got two young players, Guy Trottier and Denis Dupere, in return.

Normally, with four kids you'd be worried about uprooting them from school and moving to a new city, a new country, but the girls had reached the age — Jeri was 17 — where I thought they were old enough to really gain from the experience. I was wrong, at least at first — Kim and Kelly were miserable, skipped school as often as they attended, and made absolutely no friends. They had always had a large group of friends at home, so many that I hadn't realized how shy they both were. In the end, though, it still turned out to be a good move.

Tim was in San Francisco when he finally got the news that he had been traded to New York. I was in Pittsburgh at the time visiting my sister, and Tim called to ask me to

146

Glib promises of a broader policy on foreign takeovers...

...mere threats of preventive legislative action...

... while Canada's natural resources are ruthlessly purloined!

LEAFS' HORTON TRADED TO N.Y.

Editorial cartoon from *The Telegram* after Tim was traded to New York in the spring of 1969.

meet him in New York. When I arrived at the hotel, he was supposed to be getting some rest before the game, but it was his first game with a new team and Tim was far from his usual laid-back self.

I was on hand for Tim's first game as a Ranger. It was a loss, 2–0 to Detroit, but Tim had a super game playing alongside former Leafs Bob Nevin, Terry Sawchuk, and Rod Seiling and against Bobby Baun, Frank Mahovlich, Carl Brewer, and Pete Stemkowski. Tim played nearly 40 minutes that night, including penalty killing and the power play, and was by all accounts the best Ranger on the ice. The fans were more than happy to have Tim in the fold and things looked good with the Rangers right off the bat.

The team management arranged for Tim and I to get a suite at the Penn Garden Hotel, right across the street from Madison Square Garden at 7th and 31st. The 26th-floor suite had three bedrooms, a large living room, two baths, two balconies and a small kitchen. I liked it because it was within walking distance of just about anything worth seeing in Manhattan, and it was large enough that the girls could visit during that first few months with the team.

Tim and I had lost our dear friend Roger Pelletier just before Christmas, 1969, in a tragic accident at work and Renette and her two daughters Carole and Suzanne had become even closer over those few months. Tim made every

Telegram Sports

Horton becomes a $100,000 Ranger

SCOTT YOUNG
SPORTS EDITOR

GEORGE GROSS
ASSOCIATE SPORTS EDITOR

George Gross column from *The Telegram*, announcing Tim's first six-figure deal. Tim made good money during his last three years, but he played for peanuts during most of his time in Toronto.

effort to become a father figure for the Pelletier girls, and I think he did pretty well under the circumstances. We considered all three of them family in any case. We began spending more time together; Renette and the girls stayed at our house, and as a result the girls were able to finish their school years and I was able to spend more time with Tim in New York. In fact, Tim and I had a real New York City vacation, sightseeing, shopping, eating out. The girls, including the Pelletiers, all came down at Easter. It really was a great time for us. We were all treated very well in New York. The Rangers' organization — and the GM at the time, Emile Francis — were extremely good to the players and their families. Once, when New York was heading back to

Toronto, Francis even invited me to fly back with the team, something which would have been unheard of with the Leafs under Punch Imlach. Punch used to get angry if I was even in the same city when the Leafs were on the road.

Tim's roommate in New York that first spring was rookie defenseman Ab DeMarco:

"When it was rumoured in New York that Timmy was coming, everyone was ecstatic, and it was a big thrill for me. I had this picture on my bedroom wall at my Mom's, I mean I grew up with Timmy's picture on my wall, and now he's my roommate, and I'm going to be his defense partner! I remember after one of the first games in New York, I played about five or six shifts, so I take a shower, get dressed and I'm walking out the door after the game, and all the reporters came with their microphones crowding around Timmy. And he's just trying to get dressed, but he's being interviewed, and he sees me out of the corner of his eye and he yells, 'Ab! Where are you going?' I tell him I'm just going

Tim wore #3, his old St. Mike's number, while playing for the Rangers. Here he is covering the net in front of Ed Giacomin. Tim joined an already strong Ranger team that featured Jean Ratelle, Vic Hadfield, Bob Nevin, Rod Gilbert, and Brad Park. New York made the Stanley Cup finals that year, but lost to the Canadiens.

149

"When it was rumoured in New York that Tim was coming, everyone was ecstatic, and it was a big thrill for me. I grew up with Tim's picture on my wall, and now he was my roommate, and I was going to be his defense partner." (Ab DeMarco)

back to the hotel, and he says, 'Well wait up! I want to have a drink with you.' And I'm thinking why would Tim Horton want to have a drink with *me*? I was in awe, but sure enough he grabbed whatever he had, and we went over to the hotel and had a couple of drinks. It was a rush, just a rush."

At 41, you would think the high life would have started getting to Tim by now, but in truth, it was the younger players who had trouble keeping up with him, both on and off the ice.

"One time in my rookie year," DeMarco remembers, "Tim and Dicky Duff stayed out at El Vagabondos until five in the morning after a Sunday game, drinking Amarettos and anything else that was liquid. By that time I was at the end of the bar just hanging on with these two professional drinkers. Tim says, 'You're coming home with me!' so he throws me in the Cadillac and we go to his place. We hit a few curves on the way and it was one of the first times I grabbed a seatbelt and put it on. We get home and Tim just picks Traci up out of bed, I don't know where he put her, and he says 'You sleep here.' I guess I slept about two hours because I had to practise Monday morning. Tim didn't have to practise, but he got me up — I don't think he went to bed — and he says, 'Let's go.' So we go to the rink. I feel like a piece of crap and Timmy's doing starts and stops — he knows he has to do it because that's how he stayed in shape. There's about six or seven of us and he's passing us on the ice, and grinding us, making us do starts and stops. I mean he was 41. The man was just too strong."

Vic Hadfield, a Hall-of-Fame winger with the Rangers, was one of Tim's best friends in New York, and remembers those days fondly:

"I got to know Timmy on a close friendship basis," Vic recalls. "I couldn't have had a better friend, on or off the ice. There were trials — we would have our battles when the Leafs and the Rangers got together. Timmy was always a superstar in my eyes."

I first heard about Tim's door-crashing exploits when he was traded to the Rangers. King Clancy pulled me aside at one point to explain, and he told me: "We can afford his salary, Lori, that's fine, we just couldn't afford any more hotel doors." And so I inquired about it the next time I saw my husband.

Tim was made assistant captain his second year with the Rangers. The Rangers were a first-class organization, and treated the players and their families extremely well.

I haven't heard any door-breaking stories from the time Tim was in New York, but his nickname down there was "Superman," so I doubt very much he'd quit. Vic Hadfield does recall one prank Tim pulled after a Ranger road trip:

"When we came in late from a road game, we wouldn't get back to New York until two or three o'clock in the morning. Emile Francis would have us staying at a hotel downtown, right across from Madison Square Garden. It was an old hotel, never very busy. We were getting on the elevator to go up to our rooms late one night, and there was a Coke machine on one of the floors. So Timmy, being as strong as he was, picked up this big, six-foot Coke machine, towed it on to the elevator, and pushed the down button. Sure enough the Coke machine made it down to the main level. It would've taken fifteen of those guys to move it back, whereas Timmy could do it all by himself."

The hotel in Vic's story is the same hotel Tim and I were living in at the time, on the 26th floor. In all fairness to Tim, he had put money into that machine several times and nothing had come out. His argument later was that he had just "sent it downstairs to be repaired."

There is also a story a few Rangers tell about Brad Park waiting for Tim outside the bathroom during a plane trip and telling the flight attendant that "Superman" was "in there, changing."

We really enjoyed life in New York and Tim got to play on an excellent team — with players like Rod Gilbert and Vic Hadfield, Jean Ratelle, Ed Giacomin, and Brad Park. The Rangers did not, in fact, win the Cup that spring, but they did make it to the finals. By the end of the year Tim had ripped every phone book in the suite in half.

We visited New York a few times that summer looking for a house. We decided on Manhasset as opposed to Long Beach or Atlantic Beach where the rest of the team lived, mostly because of the school situation. We had just got settled in, the kids were in school (and hating it), when I got a phone call asking me to help out at the school Hallowe'en party. The class mother, Olga Yashinski and her husband Walter, were both from Toronto, avid hockey fans who were very anxious to meet Tim. I went to the Hallowe'en party, and back to the Yashinski house for coffee. Around 4 a.m. Walter picked up Tim at the airport,

★★★★ **FINAL** 124 | **DAILY☀NEWS** | MORE THAN TWICE THE CIRCULATION OF ANY OTHER PAPER IN AMERICA

NEW YORK'S PICTURE NEWSPAPER ®

New York, N.Y. 10017, Thursday, April 8, 1971

RANGERS GO 1-UP, WIN, 5-4
COURT NIXES FLOOD AGAIN

—Stories on Page 106

NEWS photo by Dan Farrell

Toronto's Dave Keon is a fallen Leaf and he finds himself between Rangers Brad Parks (2) and Tim Horton during a first-period scramble for the elusive puck at Madison Square Garden, where Stanley Cup playoffs began last night. They also began in Boston, Chicago, St. Louis.

Violence Grows in Garden

← Ranger goaltender Ed Giacomin more or less tends to his own business —from a ringside spot— as the gloves go off and tempers seem about to melt the Garden ice at rinkside. Eddie saw the fight, but never saw most of the pucks that flew past him last night. The Rangers beat Leafs, 5-4. *Story on page 106*

NEWS photo by Dan Farrell

Off-Track Betting—Roosevelt Selections, Entries on ↗

Tim started the playoffs in 1971 by eliminating the Leafs in the first round. It was strange for Tim to be playing against friends and teammates like Davey Keon (pictured here between Tim and Brad Park). But the move to New York rejuvenated Tim's career.

and we all had breakfast together. The four of us spent a lot of time together in New York, and Olga and I became friends. It was Olga who really introduced me to New York. Tim and I had a very active social life in New York, what with the Yashinskis, and our friends on the hockey team.

The year passed quickly. The Queripels and the Pelletiers came down for Christmas. Tim's new teammates and their wives were lovely people. There were quite a few team parties; after games we'd all go to a restaurant called El Vagabondos.

After the 1970 playoff run, Tim and his teammates were invited on a vacation down in the Bahamas. Vic Hadfield has some funny memories of that time with Tim:

"After the season, as a team we went down to Great Harbor Key [in the Bahamas] for a week to do some fishing and some golfing. Of course after the season, everybody looks like a lifeguard in a car wash — we were all so white. We all just got burnt to a crisp and I think we had to stay out of the sun for two or three days because we had severe sunburns."

"But I went fishing with Timmy, and the laughing . . . . I remember we were going to go bottom-fishing one morning after a night of quite a few cocktails. Now I'm not much of a boater and when we were about twenty-three miles out, and that old boat was just rockin', Timmy says: 'You know, you could see how somebody could get really sick here.'"

A "before and after" shot of Tim on an off-season fishing trip down south. He seems to have left his sea legs at home this trip.

"As soon as he said that, I had to bee-line right down to the washroom. I was as sick as a dog. After about five or ten minutes I came back up on to the deck. I lasted about another ten minutes . . . then back down into the washroom."

"I remember coming out of the washroom and there was a full-length mirror and I looked in the mirror — there's tears comin' out of my eyes, I'm sick as a dog — and I said to myself, 'What am I doin' here?' We just finished playing 80 or 90 hockey games and there I was, beating myself up with this stupid fishing."

"I remember going back up and telling the captain: 'Look-it, I'll buy you all the fish you want, just get me the hell back into shore!' So off we went, and as soon as we got back, I was all right — but I remember Timmy laughing like hell."

In the summer months, Tim would spend a lot of time working in the business, and whatever time he had available during the hockey season. But the business had grown to such an extent that it really required Tim's full attention. Most of Tim's indecision about playing or retiring over those last few years had little to do with his ability to play. Tim argued at one point that he could be in business his whole life, but he could only play hockey for so long.

Tim played the 1970–71 season in New York, with the intention of retiring that summer. After the season Tim and I met with Emile and he tried very hard to convince Tim to come back, but he and I had already made a decision that we were only going to stay in New York for one year. The big drawback for me at the time was that I had found a diet doctor down there who would prescribe me amphetamines, and my problem with pills had become much worse.

Knowing he would not be returning to the team, and considering Tim's age and salary, the Rangers felt safe leaving him unprotected in the expansion draft. But Tim's old teammate, Red Kelly, was now coaching in Pittsburgh, and encouraged the Penguins to claim Tim in the draft. From there, it was just a matter of convincing Tim to play another year and help out with the team's young defense. If it weren't for Red being there, or the fact that Pittsburgh was my hometown, I doubt it would have happened. Pittsburgh was home to me and I really was looking forward to being with my family for a season.

Tim was making good money by that point, and the Penguins were prepared to pay it. But when Tim went to sign his contract with Pittsburgh, he had another request. Red Kelly was present at the meeting:

"One of the things Tim wanted when he signed the contract with us was backing at the bank for his business. He already had the donut shops, several of them, but he wanted to supply those stores so he needed a warehouse and a fleet of trucks, and he couldn't get the backing of the bank. So we agreed to do that when we signed him; I knew they were successful and there wasn't going to be any danger with the loan."

I wasn't aware of this arrangement at the time, nor the fact that Tim's salary would be going directly into Tim Donut Ltd., nor did I know that the company, in turn,

If it hadn't been Red Kelly coaching the Penguins, who obtained Tim's rights in the expansion draft in 1970, Tim almost certainly would have retired. Red wanted him to work with the young Penguins' defensemen.

would be paying equal salaries to Tim and Ron Joyce. When I did find out, I was furious.

And so, when training camp came round again, Tim was out on the ice doing drills with players half his age. Red saved Tim the number 9 jersey but he refused to wear it. Nine was Gordie Howe's number — the kind of number a star player on a team would wear. He'd worn number 7 in Toronto, an unusual number for a defenseman, but only because King Clancy had asked him to wear it. But Tim never considered himself a star; he was always one player on a team, so he waited until a more "appropriate" number was available, and wore number 24. Later in the year, Tim's old St. Mike's number 3 became available, and so he wore that for the rest of the year.

On the ice, Tim was bothered by injuries during most of his stay with the Penguins. First he broke his ankle, then he badly separated a shoulder. Red Kelly has a story about the night Tim injured his shoulder.

"It was a night in Detroit, and Tim got hurt right at the end of the first period. I saw him go down, he had the puck and was about to break out and Delvecchio, who was behind him, pulled his feet out from under him and Tim landed with all his weight on his shoulder. I thought he was hurt, but Tim never gave any indication that he was. He came off, and there was just enough time left for him to have one more shift when the trainer comes over to me and says, 'Tim wants to know if it'd be okay for him to miss this one shift.' And I said, 'Okay, I thought he landed hard.'"

"We went into the dressing room and Tim went to have it looked at. When I got in there he had his shirt and his equipment off and his one shoulder was *way* out of place — I mean, it was hanging several inches off his shoulder. I asked him how he was feeling and Tim says, 'Oh, okay. I can play.' I said: 'What do you mean you can play?' And he said: 'We need this game. I can play.' We did need the game — we weren't that strong a club, and every point might make the difference between getting to the playoffs or not. But there was no way I was going to let him go out there in that condition. But that's the way Tim was. Hurt as badly as he was, he knew we needed him, that we were counting on him."

In fact, with the shoulder only partially healed, Tim had it frozen so he could play in the playoffs. But overall, the year in Pittsburgh proved awfully stressful for Tim, not being able to play half the time, and feeling he was letting his old friend down. At one point during one of his injuries he was putting away the better part of a bottle of scotch a day. He was so upset, he wasn't himself at all. He'd sit on the couch and get out his bottle of scotch and watch *Sesame Street*, and fall off his chair laughing. That was about the only entertainment Tim got that season.

Tim wasn't the only one having problems at this point, however. Shortly after I arrived in Pittsburgh, I spent two weeks in hospital and four more weeks over the course of

Tim spent all too many days in Pittsburgh at home on the couch. After being an ironman with the Leafs, going so many years without an injury, he had two major ones with the Penguins — a broken foot and a badly separated shoulder. He was so depressed at one point he was going through a bottle of scotch a day. He'd sit on the couch with a drink and watch *Sesame Street* all day.

the season mostly as a result of my substance abuse. Tim and I were fighting a lot, and every time Kim and Kelly (now teenagers) would borrow my car to go to the drugstore, they would somehow end up back in Toronto. Then Tim would have to fly up and bring them back. Eventually, we gave up and sent them both home, where their grandparents moved in to look after them.

AFTER THE SEASON ended, Tim and I took a short vacation in Puerto Vallarta, Mexico, and I had my first brush with the law. One morning Tim and I took a long ride along the coast; we were miles from anywhere and we stopped the car and went for a swim in the ocean. Well, we were

getting along beautifully and one thing led to another, until Tim suddenly noticed two men with guns, off in the distance. Turns out they were Mexican police officers; out-of-uniform, but with cocked .45s in their hands we decided not to argue about it. Their guns remained cocked as they sat behind us while we drove (on a very bumpy road) to the little jail in a nearby town. We didn't know what was happening. Tim kept trying to get them to lower their guns, saying, "Take it easy, McCloud" but we had no luck communicating with them. We spent all afternoon in jail, then someone came and collected $50 and we were released. Later, of course, Tim saw fit to share the story with everyone at the hotel.

Tim had Ken Gariepy write up a new will that summer, and he and Ron signed a share trust agreement. I wasn't to learn of these until much later.

After the miserable season in Pittsburgh, Tim decided that if he was going to retire he wasn't going to do it on such a bad note. He still had the skill to play the game, he still had the desire, the only things that concerned him as the years piled up were whether he could still perform at the level he was used to, whether he was asking too much of (and paying too much to) his partner to handle the business while he was on the ice.

Tim on a much-needed vacation with me down in Mexico, after our year in Pittsburgh. That was the trip Tim and I got a good look at the inside of a Mexican jail . . . but that's another story.

A FTER HE LEFT THE Leafs, Punch Imlach wasn't out of a job for long; he was hired on as the general manager of the expansion Buffalo Sabres. Once Punch knew Tim was not going to re-sign with the Penguins, he immediately

Tim was one of those people who could doze off at the drop of a hat. He was a great guy to travel with; you'd sit down in your seat, turn to say something to him, and he'd be fast asleep.

tried to lure Tim to Buffalo to help with a very young but talented, defense corps which included Jim Schoenfeld and Larry Carierre. Imlach treated Tim extremely well in Buffalo; it almost seemed that he was trying to make up for how badly Tim had been paid during his years with the Leafs. Punch had changed greatly from his time in Toronto. He was not under anywhere near the same amount of pressure, and the ownership in Buffalo — the Knox family — were first class in every sense of the term. Tim signed for a year with a salary of over $100,000, and the provision that he be given Mondays off to deal with the donut business in Oakville. As in Pittsburgh, Tim's salary went directly to the company in the form of a loan, and he and Ron once again were paid equally by Tim Horton Donuts.

Tim with Jimmy Schoenfeld, now an NHL coach, but a terrific defenseman for years with the Sabres. "Tim was an on-the-job tutor. Not only was he still playing extremely well, but we were still youngsters and had such great admiration for him. When he said something, we would listen." (Jim Schoenfeld)

BOB SHAVER

Tim was 42 years old when he joined the Sabres, and he was playing with teammates who were closer to his daughters' age. Tim played a more defensive style, and left most of the running around to the younger legs. But he was still the strongest player on the team.

BOB SHAVER

Schoenfeld remembers the effect of having a player of Tim's stature anchoring and teaching an eager, mobile, but very green defense:

"Tim was the greatest thing to happen to us, because he was an on-the-job tutor. Not only was he still playing extremely well, but we were still youngsters and we had such great admiration for him that when he said something, we listened. Looking back, many of the things I was taught were things I've used throughout my career, much to my benefit. It's something I think today's game misses sometimes, because the older players are overlooked in favour of younger guys and you don't have that veteran to share his experiences with you."

"I was a young kid, and throughout most of my career, I didn't sleep during the day of the game itself. I remember a time early in my first year, I would come back to my room after the pre-game meal and there's Horty lying in bed with the covers up to here, reading a book. I tried to lie down but I couldn't stay still, you know, because 'this is Tim Horton, and I'm in the room with him.' I mean I could hear myself *breathing*, and I would wonder if I was annoying him. So I said, 'I'm going to get up and go downstairs.' And Tim said, 'Well, if you're going to the gift shop, get me a bottle of Cutty Sark.' I said, 'Sure.'"

"I didn't even know what Cutty Sark was. So I went down to the gift shop and asked if they had any and the guy says 'Yeah,' and so I just hope no one sees me picking up liquor for Horty. Tim was a veteran; he knew what he needed, and I was just a kid with boundless energy. Some people would just suggest you go out somewhere or do something. Horty would just put his arm around your neck and say, 'You're coming with me,' and that's how it was. If Hort wanted you to go, you would go, without any argument at all."

"But it was fun. It was a great time. Everything was so new to me, of course Tim had been through it for twenty-two years, and it wasn't new to him — still, he had an enthusiasm for the game."

I never appreciated Tim's drinking, which over the years had moved from a recreational indulgence to a full-fledged habit. In Buffalo, Tim had really made an effort to cut down, but at times he still had real trouble with it — and his mood swings when drinking veered towards the nasty

on a couple of occasions. After one particularly ugly incident at our cottage in Huntsville after his first season in Buffalo, Tim agreed to go to a psychiatrist and see if he couldn't sort the problem out.

Tim stopped drinking the next year but he was never able to stay completely sober. His door-crashing days, however, were over. Maybe the shoulder separation a year earlier had something to do with that. But Punch had made it clear to Tim that he had been brought in to serve as an example to the younger players, and Tim behaved accordingly.

Because Tim was making an honest effort to stop drinking, I had cut my pill consumption down to one a day. I had already been hospitalized (unsuccessfully) twice for substance abuse, but the addiction was so strong I knew I was going to need more professional help to stop completely. For some reason neither of us had heard of AA, but I think now that the organization could have helped us change the course of our lives.

O UR FIRST WINTER in Buffalo we lived in Fort Erie in a beautiful house on the lake. It was large enough for the girls to visit once again; Jeri and Carole were there often and Traci and a girlfriend would come down on school holidays. Kim and Kelly were never big hockey fans, and so preferred to stay in Toronto with their crowd. I was home every weekend, Tim would visit the office on Mondays, and he would be home by four in the afternoon when the girls got home from school. We'd have dinner, watch some TV, and leave for Buffalo when *Laugh-In* was over. Tim would leave Tuesday night for a Wednesday evening game, return Wednesday night, and leave again Friday night.

This was our routine both years we were in Buffalo. I never attended the Sunday night games, instead watching

Tim with my co-author, Tim Griggs, in his younger days. Tim would spend a harrowing evening baby-sitting his godson a year or two later.

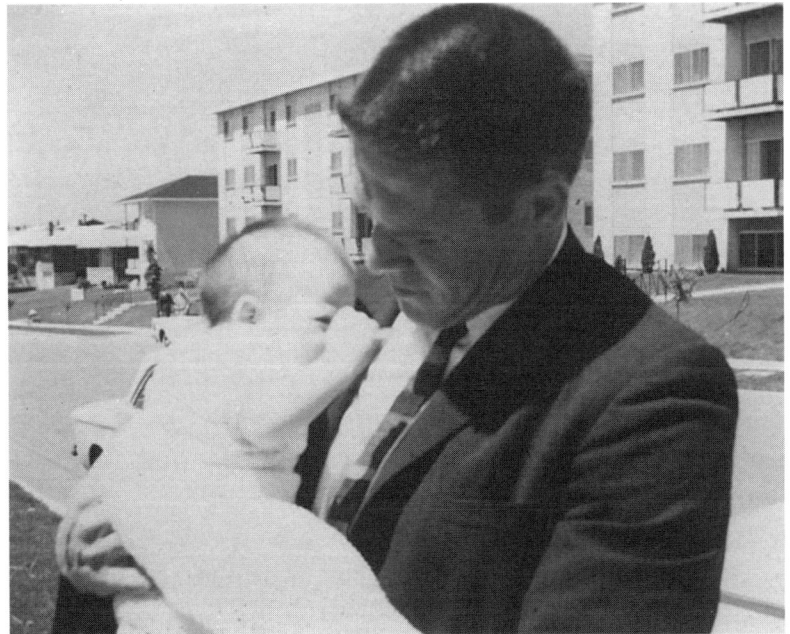

them on TV in Toronto. When Tim was away he spoke to the girls daily on the phone, and sometimes more often, as he always had.

But Tim was certainly home more often, even finding the time on one occasion to dabble in babysitting. I don't know whether he was just out of practice, but Tim's godson Tim Griggs tells a story about an afternoon his uncle Tim ran into trouble babysitting himself and his two brothers:

"I was only two at the time so I only vaguely remember, but I've been told the story a million times. It's a family story. My Mum and Dad were going somewhere and needed a babysitter for the kids. Tim offered to babysit, Lori and the girls were going out, so it was Tim babysitting my two brothers, Jim and Joe, and myself, at their place on Bannatyne. Things were going fine, we were all in the swimming pool in the backyard, but then I took off inside the house and closed and locked the sliding patio doors. I jumped up on the kitchen counter, which was right beside the door, and while Tim was trying to open the door, I sat up there with the vegetable sprayer, spraying him out the kitchen window. The more I sprayed him the madder he got."

"I'm not sure what happened, but eventually I must have let him in. I don't know what Tim did after that to keep us in line, but when everybody got back to Tim's place, when they walked in there was Tim passed out on the couch, with two of us under one arm, and one under the other. Me and my brother Joe were both asleep, and my oldest brother Jim was just balling his eyes out because he couldn't believe how bad his brother had been. Tim never offered to babysit again."

Tim always had a way with children; he would go out of his way to share a word with them or sign an autograph. Tim Griggs recalls one afternoon when a visit from his uncle Tim turned into a neighbourhood event:

"I would have been six at the time, and Tim and Lori were coming down to see us. We weren't supposed to tell anyone that Tim was coming. If we wanted to bring one or two friends over to meet Tim, that was fine, but we were told that they were here socially, so we weren't to tell everyone. My brothers and I promised we wouldn't. But by the time he arrives, sure enough, there was a line-up of about 200 kids in our driveway — it looked like every kid in town was there. But Tim came out, threw me up on his shoulders, and we must have been out there for over an hour, saying hello and signing autographs for them."

Of course, kids are not above exploiting family connections from time to time. When we were living in Willowdale, we'd caught Traci selling pictures of her father door-to-door for a dime apiece. And Tim Griggs

One of a few dozen autographs requested by young Joe Griggs. The inscription reads "Joe. Best wishes to a Ken Dryden fan, your old uncle Tim."

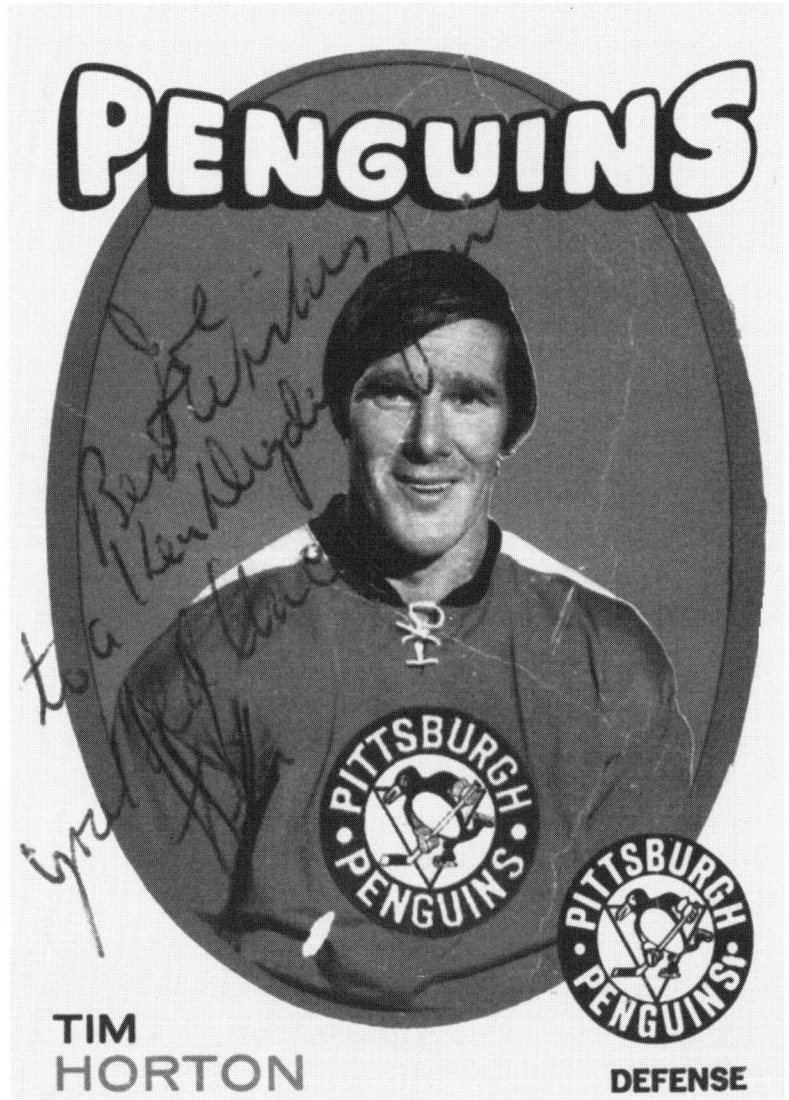

PENGUINS

TIM HORTON

DEFENSE

remembers his brother Joe had a scheme of his own going at one point:

"As kids, of course we were into collecting hockey cards," Tim recalls. "And of course, we would collect Tim Horton. I was only eight when he was killed, so I really didn't have any idea of his magnitude as a hockey player. As far as I was concerned he was my old uncle Tim who played in the NHL. But just the same, you'd get his card in a pack and you'd say, 'There he is, there's uncle Tim!' And we'd pull all his cards out so when he and Lori would come and visit, we could get him to autograph them."

"My brother Joe was two years older than me and he as really into collecting cards — much more than I was. Once when Tim and Lori were over, Joe came out with three or four more hockey cards, and Tim got to thinking while he was signing them. So he asked Joe, 'What are you doing with all these hockey cards? Why do you want so many of them signed?' And so Joe tells him, 'Well, I found out I could get one Ken Dryden card for two Tim Horton autographed cards.' Tim's reaction was, 'Oh yeah. Everybody loves Ken. Nobody loves me!' Years later, Joe ran into Ken at an autograph session, and when he told him the story they both had a good laugh about it."

Tim on the ice with one of the Sabres' apprentice defensemen, Paul Terbenche. Paul roomed with Tim on the road: "What we really enjoyed doing was talking. We used to stroll through the cities and have gab sessions. You spend some time on the road with a guy like that and you really find things out."
BOB SHAVER

Athletes rise above it all!

• TIM HORTON

I JUST can't allow Iris Nowell to get away with the garbage she wrote (Sunday Sun, Nov. 4).

Being married to a superb professional athlete for a happy 22 years and being closely associated with many others, I can only say — Don't worry parents, your children's heroes are being slandered, but they are all man enough to rise above it.

And Dr. Timpson sounds suspiciously like a frustrated athlete.

Mrs. Tim Horton,
Willowdale

PS: Being the daughter of a professional athlete for 21 years, I must agree that Ms. Nowell's research wasn't very exhaustive.

Ms. Jeri Horton

• JERI & LORI HORTON

Read it and weep, sports fans, The sexual athlete's a loser!

At least according to eelance writer Iris Nowell, who even suggests, after some exhaustive search, that truck drivers may have the edge in bed.

From last week's Sunday Sun

The Sunday Sun, November 11, 1973 **11**

A little bit of fun Jeri and I had with an article published in the *Toronto Sun*. I felt I had to defend my husband from such slanderous attacks.

This is Tim getting his team MVP award from Sabres owner Seymour Knox after the 1970–71 season. The Sabres have a very strong alumni, and the players from those years meet regularly and are still very close. Any time the team invites me back to Buffalo, I go. I would just hate to miss anything.

T IM CONTINUED HIS habit of inviting the single guys over for dinner while he was in Buffalo — Jimmy Schoenfeld and Gil Perreault were frequent guests and we all became good friends. Tim was 43 at this point, and most of the players' wives were closer in age to my kids than they were to us. Tim was only a year younger than his coach, Joe Crozier.

"You know, when Punch first told me he was going to sign Tim, I was a little leery," Crozier remembers. "But everything he did, he was the best at. If he came on the ice to do sprints, he'd be first at it. We were a team with a lot of young lads and it's hard to describe what Tim did for us as a team. Schoenfeld thought the world of him, without a doubt. Everything was Tim, Tim, Tim. I remember Jimmy breaking his leg and then asking me if he could make the trip with us to the West Coast. And I thought, 'What the hell are we bringing this guy for?' But then Timmy comes into me and says, 'Crow, I think we should take Schoenfeld and he can play the guitar.' And sure enough, Jim brought the guitar and he played in the airports and he played everywhere for us. We were a close group; we were young but we were a good hockey club."

During Tim's first year with the Sabres, Imlach's hastily assembled group of rookies and hand-picked veterans made a late season surge that must have reminded Tim of the miracle finish 15 years back. For years, expansion teams would be the doormats of the league, but Imlach's Sabres reached respectability well ahead of schedule. In Tim's first year as a Sabre — only the third season in the team's history, the Sabres beat the St. Louis Blues to gain a playoff spot

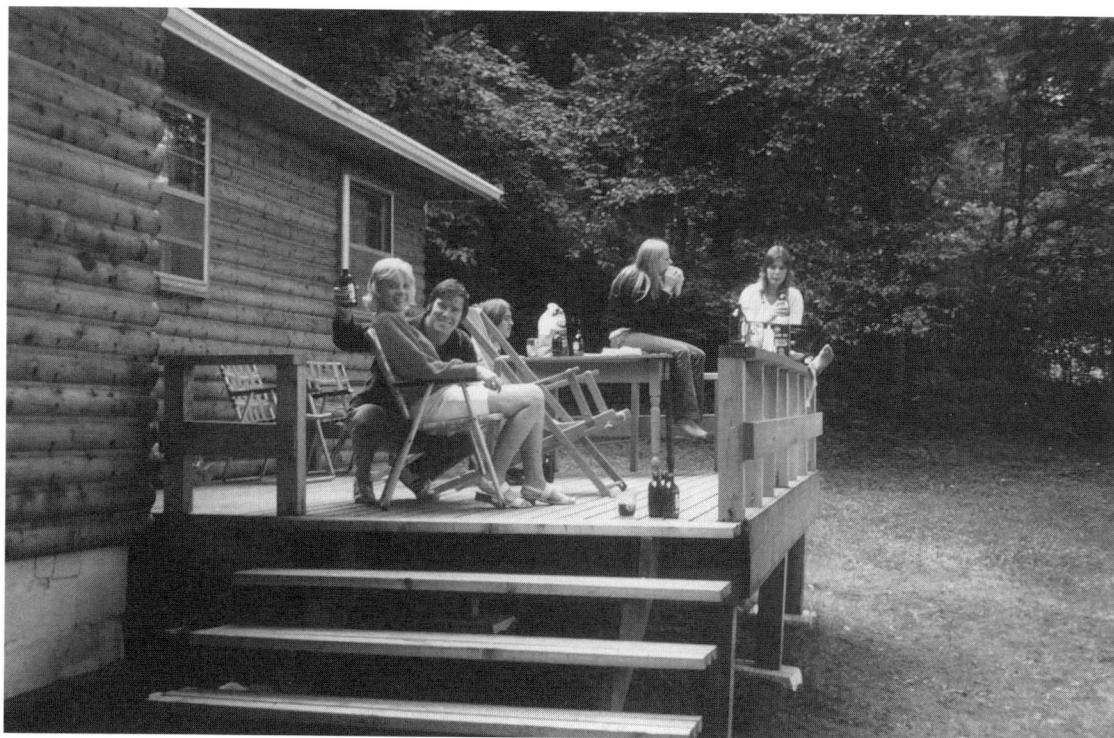

on the last night of the season. In the first round of the playoffs, they even gave the mighty Canadiens a scare before bowing out. After that final game of the 1972–73 season, the players left the ice to chants of "Thank You, Sabres." Buffalo has always had great fans.

Tim was named the MVP for the Sabres that year, his 22nd in the National Hockey League, and he was sure at that time that he had played his last game.

WE HAD PURCHASED a cottage just outside Huntsville and had done quite a big renovation on it. Tim and the girls loved it there. We opened it up with a family reunion (my family, Tim's idea) and the first week we moved in there were 34 people there. Tim took long weekends all summer to finish the work that still needed to be done and Sid Queripel brought his crew up to do the landscaping. It was a great summer for the most part, and, as it turned out, the only summer Tim had to enjoy it.

Imlach, who said at the time he thought Tim could play *two or three* more years, approached him to play again at the

The summer of 1973 we purchased a cottage on a lake just outside Huntsville. Tim loved it up there and spent most of that summer renovating the place with friends and family. Unfortunately, it was the only year Tim had to enjoy it. Whenever Kim has a nice dream about Tim she calls me, and in the dreams they're always sitting on this porch talking.

Tim in our first boat, which we bought in Fort Erie and took up to the cottage in Huntsville. When we first got it up there, the water was too low to launch the boat. The markers weren't even in yet, but Tim put it in anyway. We got about 100 feet before scraping bottom.

end of the summer. This time Tim declined, telling him he "just didn't know" whether he could still do the job on the ice. The Sabres started training camp, and worked their way through most of the pre-season games without Tim. After a 5–2 pre-season pounding from the Pittsburgh Penguins prompted a "We want Horton!" chant among the Sabres fans, Imlach set up another meeting in St. Catharines and

Tim used to say that he was paid for practices, and played the games for nothing. Even at his age, Tim outworked most of his teammates. "Everything he did, he was the best at. If he came out on the ice to do sprints, he'd be first at it. We were a close group. We were young, but we were a good hockey club." (Joe Crozier)

offered Tim $150,000 — six times what he'd been making most of his years in Toronto. Tim asked Imlach to throw in a Ford De Tomaso Pantera — a new, Italian-built sports car — and he had himself a deal. When the regular season began, Tim had himself a new car, and was back on the blue line with the Sabres.

In an article by Rick Johnston of the *Buffalo Evening News* which appeared in the Sabres program early in the season, Tim explained his reasons for coming back for one more year: "It honestly wasn't the money," he said. "We had all that worked out. Maybe it's just a bad habit I've acquired. I like to play hockey. I have a long time ahead to sit behind a desk."

Though he had lost a step, even at his age Tim was one of the best skaters on the team. His game was so sound fundamentally, and Tim was so strong in the corners that he was still a valuable asset on the ice for any NHL team. "That's the thing about Horton," Imlach commented in the same article. "You know when he goes into the corner with someone from the opposition, that guy isn't going to come out with the puck. It's just as true now as it was in his best days with the Leafs."

During an interview one night on Punch's pre-game radio show, Tim suggested he could probably play his game in a rocking chair on the ice. He had consciously changed his style so that he played a more defensive role, and allowed his young defense partners to rush the puck and join the offense.

Tim at a charity softball tournament with the St. Catharines fire-fighters in 1972. When he played the outfield, Tim couldn't see a thing. But he could hit the heck out of the ball.
THE STANDARD, ST. CATHARINES

Paul Terbenche (on the day of our interview) sitting next to Jeri at her and Ron Joyce Jr.'s Tim Horton store in Cobourg.

Tim checking the Montreal puck-carrier as Canadiens' great (and current New Jersey Devils coach) Jacques Lemaire moves into the slot for the pass, 1972–73 season.

BOB SHAVER

"As you get older," Tim told Bob Dunn of the Montreal *Star*, "you get lazier. You stay back a little more. I don't think I've passed centre ice all winter. It's kinda nice."

Tim's roommate on the road that first year, and a very good friend through Tim's time in Buffalo, was young defenseman Paul Terbenche. Terbenche confirmed that Tim wasn't doing much drinking at that point, so the two of them spent a lot of time walking:

"What we really enjoyed doing was talking," he recalls. "We used to stroll through the cities and have gab sessions. . . . He used to talk a lot about [Lori] and the girls. . . . You spend some time on the road and you really find things out." Paul was having problems on and off the ice at the time, and Tim really took him under his wing.

Tim was on a real Vitamin E kick at the time — he'd found out about it in Toronto — and he used to take five or six thousand units a day. The way Tim thought, if taking one tablet was good then ten would be better. Tim had an extremely strong heart. The doctors at Sunnybrook Hospital did a study of him during the years he was in Toronto, and they told him he had the perfect athlete's heart; it didn't speed up much when he exercised, his heart rate always stayed just about the same.

During his second year in Buffalo, Tim and I had an apartment at the Statler Hilton in Buffalo, directly across the hall from Punch and Dodo Imlach's suite. Tim would walk by and bang on Punch's door every night to let him know what time he'd gotten in. The Statler was the same hotel used by visiting teams when they came into town to play the Sabres. So Tim's old friends — now scattered all over the league — would drop upstairs and visit with us as soon as they had the chance.

Tim was on the road and I was home just about two weeks before Christmas 1973. It was the first year the NHL had decided it would no longer schedule any hockey games on Christmas Day. On the Friday before Christmas, Renette and I were busy decorating and preparing food for the Christmas Eve party, and it was the first year since Roger's death that Renette seemed to be able to enjoy herself on Christmas. We were all decorating the tree, when Tim walks in, completely unexpected (by everyone except Renette). Tim had a few hours before catching the train for a

Still playing at 44. "As you get older, you get lazier. You stay back a little more. I don't think I've passed centre ice all winter. It's kinda nice."

BOB SHAVER

Gil Perreault was one of the most exciting players ever to play in the NHL, and one of my favorite people. Here he awaits the drop pass from Tim that will begin one of his trademark end-to-end rushes.

BOB SHAVER

pre-Christmas game against Montreal, and he'd taken a cab home to surprise us. For many years Christmas was an awkward time for us; Tim was often on the road playing a game and Santa Claus usually had to come a few days early. For Tim to be there with us while we trimmed the tree really made the evening. Tim flew back for Christmas Day

Tim with my mother at a wedding in the early 1970s. My mother never saw a sporting event in her whole life, but she loved Tim. One night in Pittsburgh I showed up for the game and there was my mother sitting in the stands. When Tim came out on the ice, he looked up and his jaw dropped. We tried to explain the game to her, but after about ten minutes she said: "If the goal is to put the puck in the nets, why are those two guys standing there?"

and we all had a wonderful holiday. I really haven't had a great Christmas since; the arrival of my grandchildren has helped a lot, but it has never been the same.

Tim lost his father in January 1974, and Ethel came down and traveled to Florida with me and my sisters, then visited for about ten days in Buffalo. Tim came in on Valentine's Day with a huge floral arrangement for each of us. She and I drove back to Toronto on a Friday to meet Gerry, who was coming down that week to take his mother back home to North Bay.

Some time over the next few days Tim caught a puck in the face during a team practice. He was pretty sure he'd broken something, but the initial diagnosis was that he had suffered a cracked jaw. Tim scheduled an appointment with the team doctor for X-rays in Buffalo, but in the meantime, the Sabres had a Wednesday game in Toronto against the Leafs. After he had kissed us all goodbye, Kelly ran after her father and hugged and kissed him again, telling him that she loved him. It was an impulse that has haunted Kelly

The 1973–74 Buffalo Sabres. The goalies are Dave Dryden and Roger Crozier. The offense was led by the famed "French Connection" line: René Robert (standing above Tim), Richard Martin (first from left in second row), and Hall of Famer Gil Perreault (next to Crozier, front right). Jim Schoenfeld is standing behind captain Gerry Meehan in the second row.

Our time in Buffalo allowed us to get to know some of my relatives. These are my cousins Ceil and Ruth, and Ruth's husband, taken just a week before Tim's death.

over the years since — she had never done that before.

Tim's face was swelling and he was in a lot of pain. With the help of painkillers, he was able to play the first two periods, but after that he was just too sore to continue. The Sabres lost the game, 4–2, but despite all his discomfort, Tim played well enough to be selected as one of the game's three stars. Tim was examined by the trainers, took some more painkillers for his jaw, talked to Punch and Dodo Imlach and his old friend Davey Keon.

Tim was supposed to have had a meeting with a business friend at George's Spaghetti House but for some reason the guy didn't show up. Before he left the building, he told Davey he was going to drive around and look for the girls. I stayed home that night with Tim's mother, but all four of the girls, their cousin Kerry, Renette, and Gerry went down to watch Tim play. After the game, the girls went to meet their father and see how he was, but they must have been waiting at the wrong exit, because for some reason they missed each other. The girls actually did see Tim's car, driving by at one point, but Tim failed to spot them.

Tim had come up from Buffalo by car early to see his mother, so he had planned to drive back rather than travel with the rest of the team by bus. When he couldn't find the girls, he headed directly to Oakville and stopped in at the office to sign some papers. Later, Ron was driving by and saw the lights on and Tim's car out front so he stopped in as well. Tim and Ron sat and talked for hours, because he called me at 3:00 in the morning, and also talked to his brother. Gerry recognized that Tim had been drinking, and he tried to convince him to stay where he was. Ron even offered to have Tim stay with him. Some time around 3:30 in the morning, Tim left the office and set out for Buffalo.

A little after 4:00 a.m. a woman reported to the OPP in Burlington that she had been passed at a very high speed on the QEW, and officers were advised on the police radio to watch out for a speeding car. At about 4:30, some 35 miles down the road, St. Catharines policeman Mike Gula was passed by a Ford Pantera traveling in excess of 100 miles per hour. Gula pulled his cruiser onto the highway and gave chase.

At 5:30 Joe Crozier was woken up by a phone call:

"We were laying in bed and the damn phone rang. First

176

Several hours after this picture was taken Tim Horton (No. 2 at right) was killed in car crash on the Q.E.

Miles Gilbert (Tim) Horton

Buffalo defenceman dies when car crashes

ST. CATHARINES (CP) — Tim Horton, 44-year-old defence star with Buffalo Sabres of the National Hockey League, was killed early yesterday when his sports car ran off the Queen Elizabeth Way at more than 100 miles an hour.

Horton was thrown from the car as it flipped over several times and was pronounced dead at the scene.

Horton presumably was on his way to Buffalo after playing with the Sabres in an NHL game against the Maple Leafs in Toronto Wednesday night. Although the Sabres lost 4-2, Horton was selected as one of the game's three stars.

Constable Mike Gula of the St. Catharines police detachment said a sports car passed him on the Queen Elizabeth Way about 4:30 at a high speed. Constable Gula said he gave chase and clocked the car at "over 100 miles an

hour. The car was identified as an Italian-built Ford Pantera.

The speed limit on that section of the highway is 60 mph. The car left the highway, went on to a grass median which is about 15 feet wide, rolled over several times and ended up in the westbound lane.

Horton's body was found 123 feet from the car.

He had been travelling alone and weather conditions were clear and dry.

Officers were advised by police radio to be on the lookout for a speeding car after a motorist told Ontario Provincial Police at Burlington that a car passed him at high speed.

The speeding car passed Constable Gula's cruiser about 35 miles later, near the Lake Street exit from the Queen Elizabeth Way at St. Catharines.

A native of Cochrane where he was christened Miles Gilbert, Horton was selected to NHL all-star teams six times —three on the first team and three on the second. He was coaxed out of retirement just before the start of this season by Buffalo general manager Punch Imlach, who had been his coach for many seasons in Toronto.

Imlach said during last fall's contract negotiations with Horton that money was not the main obstacle. At Horton's age, the veteran defenceman was not sure whether he could physically endure another NHL season.

Another factor was the growing business interests of Horton, who owned a chain of more than 30 doughnut shops in Ontario. A strong skater with a powerful shot, Horton played his final years as an amateur with Toronto St. Michael's Colege in the Ontario Hockey Association Junior A

series. He turned professional with Pittsburgh Hornets of the American Hockey League in the 1949-50 season and also appeared in one game with the Maple Leafs in that campaign.

His first full season with Toronto was in 1952-53.

He played with Toronto until March 3, 1970, when he was sent to New York Rangers for forwards Guy Trottier and Denis Dupere. He was drafted by Pittsburgh Penguins of the NHL from New York in the intra-league draft on June 3, 1971, and then was drafted by Buffalo from Pittsburgh on June 5, 1972.

Prior to this season, Horton had appeared in 1,391 games, scoring 115 goals and 397 assists. He played in 126 playoff games, with 11 goals and 39 assists.

Horton was selected to the first NHL All-Star team in 1963-64, 1967-68 and 1968-69. He was named to the second All-Star team in 1953-54, 1962-63 and 1966-67.

Horton played on four Stanley Cup winners with Toronto, all coached by Imlach—1961-62, 1962-63, 1963-64 and 1966-67.

He leaves his wife, Lori, and four daughters.

CP wire story reporting Tim's death. The newspapers knew about Tim's accident hours before I did. Dodo Imlach was the one who broke the news by calling to express her sorrow. The whole thing was handled badly, but I guess there's no good way to get this kind of news.

TORONTO STAR

THE crampled wreckage of Tim Horton's exotic sportscar. The Ford Pantera flipped at high speed on the Queen Elizabeth Way as Horton was en route from Toronto to F

The remains of Tim's Pantera. Even at the speed he was going (about 130 mph), he might have had a chance if he'd been wearing his seat belt. In a bizarre twist of fate, a couple of years ago the OPP officer who was chasing Tim at the time died on the same stretch of road. He'd pulled over a speeder and was hit by a passing car.

TORONTO STAR PHOTO

thing they said was 'This is OPP in St. Catharines. Are you Joe Crozier, the coach of the Sabres?' I told him yes and he said, 'We have one of your players here and we want you to come down here and get him.' "

At that time most of the Sabres players lived in Fort Erie, and, as Joe's wife Bonnie recalls, her husband's first reaction was that some of the players might have been out drinking and gotten into trouble: "But the officer says, 'No, no, Joe. There's been an accident.' And Joe asked right away, 'Who is it?' And he said, 'It's Tim Horton.' That's when we connected that it was not a fight, that it was Tim and he was hurt, and it was a shock. The guy says, 'Joe, are you still there? He's hurt, I need you here,' and Joe said, 'Well, okay, I'll be there right away.' Then the officer told him, 'Joe, he's hurt badly.' And Joe asks 'How badly?' And then he said 'Joe, I need you to identify the body.' "

Joe's initial reaction was that he had to get word to Punch Imlach. But at the time Joe was afraid to tell him, and it occurred to both Joe and Bonnie that a mistake could have been made, or that Tim might have loaned his car to someone. Joe and Bonnie called John Butch, the team doctor and a close friend.

"When we got to St. Catharines," Bonnie remembers, "the OPP were waiting for us. The three of us went in, and there on the desk was a pair of black glasses. And that's when I knew it was him. And you know what you hope for — somebody else driving his car. But right then we just knew."

Tim's car had skidded off the road near the Lake Street

178

exit and rolled several times before coming to a rest across the median in the westbound lanes. Timmy was thrown from the car and died instantly. The police found his body well over a hundred feet from the wreck.

After the shock of seeing their friend dead, Joe, Bonnie and John needed a place to sit down and collect their thoughts. They ended up at a Tim Hortons.

"We must have looked like three zombies," Bonnie recalls. "The girl came up and recognized Joe and said, 'Boy, my boss played one hell of a game tonight.' And all Joe could say was, 'Yes. He did.'"

By rights the police should have notified the family right after the body was identified. Joe and Bonnie called a friend right away and asked him if he would get word to Punch and to us.

There's no good way to receive this kind of news, but the first I heard of the accident was early that morning when Punch's wife Dodo called me to express her condolences. And then the phone started ringing off the hook. The girls had their own phone upstairs, and they found out the same way, before I had a chance to break it to them, when their own friends heard about it on the radio and called. Jeri was working for Air Canada at the airport that morning and was completely oblivious to her father's death. Some of her co-workers had heard, but it was 9 a.m. before the supervisor found the nerve to tell her.

It turns out the OPP called Joe because they found a piece of paper in Tim's wallet with Joe's name and phone number on it, and it was the only number they had. But they never called me. In fact, the police did not show up to tell me what happened until 2:00 that afternoon, and even then they told Gerry and not me. I guess they didn't want to tell me themselves.

There's no doubt that side of it was handled badly, but really it made no difference to me. There's no good time to hear news like that. I just felt so sorry for Dodo when she realized I hadn't heard and that she would have to tell me.

THE WORD ABOUT TIM's accident spread quickly among his teammates. Jim Schoenfeld was among the first to hear the sad news:

The Toronto Star ⟨C⟩ SPOI

SECTION C—PAGES C1 TO C8   FRIDAY, FEBRUARY 22, 1974   ★

—Star photo by D

TEARS FOR A TEAMMATE: Jim Schoenfeld (second from right) weeps unashamedly at Buffalo Memorial Auditorium last night as Buffalo Sabres stand with heads bowed, observing minute of silence in memory of Tim Horton, who died in car crash early yes Other Sabres, all with black arm bands, are (left to right) Farr, Larry Carriere and Craig Ramsay. Sabres tied Atlan

Jimmy and his mates during the minute of silence observed at the Sabres game the night after Tim died. "There was a minute of silence and it was like I felt everyone's loss all at once, how the whole community felt about Tim . . . and suddenly there I was, crying to start the game." (Jim Schoenfeld)

DON DUTTON, TORONTO STAR

180

"We got a call in the morning that he died," Jimmy remembers. "We were living in Fort Erie at the time. When we first came to the team, everybody lived on the Canadian side. Teresa and I were married at that point and staying in the beach house. There was no one near us for perhaps a half-mile radius because all the other people went back to Buffalo for the winter. It was just us and the dog when I got the news that Timmy left that morning."

"I remember walking the dog on the beach and of course it was all snow and ice at the time. You try and reconcile things in your mind, and I remember I just went over and shoveled snow. Just to do something, you know, just shovel it from one place to another."

"I thought I was fine. I went to the game and it was funny; standing there for the national anthem, there was a minute of silence and it was like I felt everyone else's loss all at once, how the whole community felt about Tim and, Christ, suddenly there I was, crying to start the game. When I came to the bench, I was saying 'I'm fine, I'm fine.' But, of course, I wasn't. It's funny how you think you have a grasp on your emotions."

In a Dick Johnston article which ran on Friday the 22nd in the *Buffalo Evening News*, Paul Terbenche described how strange it was to play a game knowing you'd just lost a teammate and friend. "It just seemed as though I wasn't there at the start of the game," Paul said. "During the game I'd forget what had happened. I would look up and expect to see Tim beside me, at defense, but he wasn't there. He wasn't anywhere. The more I worked the more I forgot and just played hockey. But then it all came back after the game."

Sabres captain Gerry Meehan was also broken up. He'd had a day of mixed emotions, hearing of Tim's death within a few minutes of finding out his wife, Mirella, had just given birth to their second child (they later named the child Tim). Don Luce, who had also played with Tim in New York, could barely bring himself to speak in a subdued

CITY OF BUFFALO
OFFICE OF THE MAYOR

STANLEY M. MAKOWSKI
MAYOR

February 22, 1974

Mrs. Miles G. Horton
105 Bannatyne Drive
Willowdale, Ontario

Dear Mrs. Horton:

Please allow me to express my deepfelt loss at the tragic news of Tim's accident. Everyone is deeply stunned as I know you and the children must be.

As Mayor of Buffalo, I want you to know that Tim was held in very high esteem, not only as an outstanding figure in the world of sports but as a valuable and respected member of this community.

To me, Tim was a fine man, a true gentleman and a great athlete. I will never forget the occasion when I met him personally and was unforgettably impressed by his thoughtfulness when he mentioned you to me.

I feel a true personal loss in Tim's untimely and dreadfully tragic death. I realize it serves as little comfort to you at this time, but while I pray for Tim I also pray that God will provide to his family the strength and the spiritual guidance to bear this cross and I offer thanks that we were blessed with Tim's presence for the years he was with us.

Sincerely,

Stanley M. Makowski
Stanley M. Makowski

A letter of condolence from Buffalo Mayor Stanley Makowski.

LAST FAREWELL: Carrying Tim Horton's casket to burial plot in York Cemetery yesterday are pall bearers (clockwise) ... Armstrong and Dick Duff—all former Maple Leaf teammates of Horton, who was killed in one-car crash last Thursday on ... cluding fans as well as present and former teammates hockey officialdom, squeezed into Oriole-York Mills Un... Church for funeral service and overflowed into church basem...

—Star photo by Ro...

The pallbearers at the funeral were all Tim's teammates from the Stanley Cup winners in Toronto: Dave Keon, Bobby Baun, Allan Stanley, Billy Harris, George Armstrong, and Dicky Duff. There were also over a dozen honourary pallbearers and there could easily have been more — Tim just had so many close, close friends.

Sabres' dressing room. "I played [tonight] for him," Luce told reporters. He'd scored two goals in leading the Sabres back from a 4–1 deficit to a 4–4 tie.

I REMEMBER THOSE next few days only vaguely. The funeral was held on the following Monday at Oriole-York Mills United Church. Twelve hundred people attended the service, including the whole Sabres team, and virtually all of the players from Tim's Leafs days. As a Toronto *Sun* article noted the next day, the list of friends and former teammates at the service "read like roll call of hockey's great names." There was NHL president Clarence Campbell, former coaches Joe Primeau, King Clancy, Punch Imlach, and Joe Crozier; Harold Cotton, Ron Ellis, Red Wing captain Red Berenson, Carl Brewer, Harold Ballard, Bob Goldham, and Gus Bodnar.

The pallbearers were some of Tim's closest friends from the Stanley Cup years — George Armstrong, Allan Stanley, Dave Keon, Dick Duff, Billy Harris, and Bobby Baun. Honourary pallbearers included Punch Imlach, Dickie Moore, Red Kelly, Jim Schoenfeld, Paul Terbenche, Joe Crozier, Eddie Shack, King Clancy, Sid Queripel, Bryan Watson, Bill Landon, Ken Gariepy, and Larry Mann. I knew these were the people that Tim loved dearly. I probably missed some, but it was a difficult time.

Jim Schoenfeld describes the effect that day had on him: "You know, seeing Timmy in the casket, if there was anyone who shouldn't have been in one it was Horty. It was funny how as a young man I was looking down and thought, 'I'm going to get cremated.' It just changes your whole way of thinking. But to me that wasn't even Horty. Horty looked like, you know, 'Get me out of this thing.' It's strange the effect that things have on you. The whole thing, it just didn't fit his personality. He was sort of uncontainable. You really couldn't contain Horty."

I don't remember too much from that day, beyond laying the flowers on the casket and the girls saying goodbye. I do remember that a number of officers of the Buffalo police department came up for the funeral and served as an honour guard — they were the people who controlled traffic around the Auditorium in Buffalo and who'd come to know Tim over the years as a friend. Hundreds of Toronto policemen also worked on their days off, controlling the crowd. Frank and Marie Mahovlich came down on the Saturday, which was a game night for Frank, just so they could be there. The eulogy was delivered by Reverend Gord Griggs.

The amount of mail I received at that time expressing sorrow at Tim's passing was overwhelming. There was a lovely letter from Jean and Seymour Knox. There were official condolences from the city of Toronto and the Mayor of Buffalo. There were letters from teammates and friends and people who used to run restaurants where Tim would eat. There was even a letter from the speaker of the House of Assembly of Newfoundland, which passed on a unanimous resolution of sympathy for the people of Newfoundland, who had received us so well on our trip to St. John's years earlier. And there were letters and cards from kids — a lot of those.

In fact, it was probably too overwhelming for me at the time. I moved from our old house on Bannatyne in 1983. When I moved into a new

IN REMEMBERANCE

M.G. (Tim) Horton

Memorial card from the funeral. I can't remember a whole lot from those few days. I remember laying flowers on the casket, and the girls saying goodbye. But I was in a daze, really.

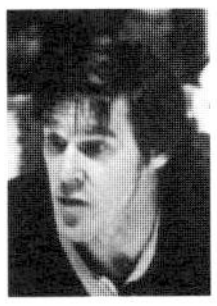

Kidder, Peabody & Co.
Incorporated
1122 MARINE TRUST BUILDING
BUFFALO, N.Y. 14203

Feb. 21, 1974

Dear Lori;
I just cannot tell you how shocked Jean & I were early this morning to hear the tragic news of Tim's accident. We are all at ~~a~~ loss for words to express our disbelief and sorrow to you and your four lovely daughters.
I had come to know Tim somewhat better than most of our other players during this season and can assure you he was one of my friends. I have always had the utmost of respect and admiration for Tim as a person and as

THE HOUSE OF ASSEMBLY OF THE PROVINCE
OF NEWFOUNDLAND AND LABRADOR
THE SPEAKER
ST. JOHN'S

February 27, 1974.

Mrs. Lauri Horton and family,
c/o Maple Leaf Gardens,
TORONTO, ONTARIO.

Dear Mrs. Horton:

The Newfoundland House of Assembly at its sitting on Friday, February 22nd., 1974, unanimously passed the following Resolution, which was moved by the Honourable T.A. Hickman, Acting Premier and Minister of Justice, and seconded by the Honourable the Leader of the Opposition, Mr. Edward M. Roberts:

'BE IT RESOLVED that this House place on record its sense of the great loss to the world of Hockey as the result of the untimely and tragic death of Mr. Tim Horton. Newfoundland remembers well, and with affection, the visits that Mr. Horton made to this Province, and the courage and leadership he showed and the example he passed on to the young people of Newfoundland'.

On behalf of all the Members of the House of Assembly, and on my own behalf, sincerest sympathy is extended to all relatives of the bereaved.

Yours sincerely,

James Russell

James Russell,
Speaker,
House of Assembly of Newfoundland.

Letter from Seymour Knox and his wife. So many people sent their condolences after Tim died: friends, teammates, people who knew him, and kids — there were a lot from kids. It took me twenty years to open some of them — it was just overwhelming for me at the time.

Another touching letter — this one from the Speaker of the House on behalf of the Newfoundland legislature.

At the Hall-of-Fame dinner with Eddie Shack and Harold Ballard. Tim always got along well with Harold and so did I. But I didn't see much of him in his later years. Eddie has been a rock to me over the years — he has a heart as big as himself.

HOCKEY HALL OF FAME

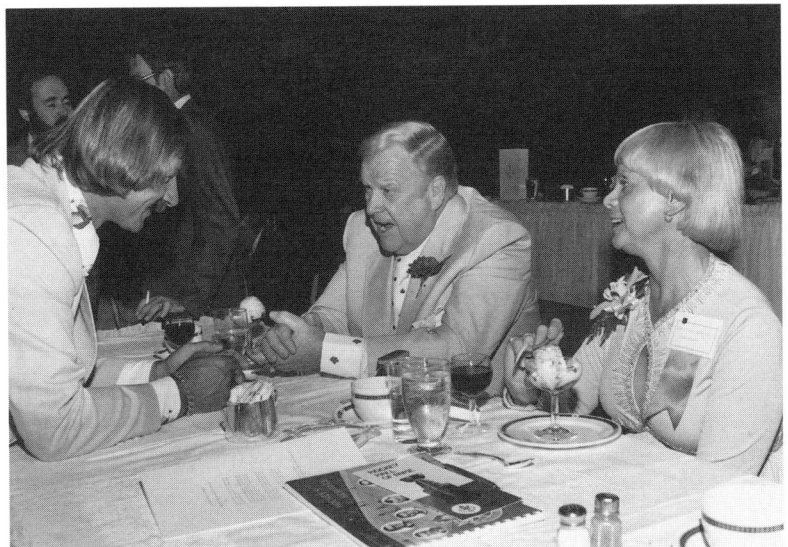

A Tribute to Tim

The following from an anonymous 15-year-old girl hockey fan, printed without editing or correction, is a touching and reassuring tribute to Tim Horton, Buffalo Sabre defenseman killed last week in an automobile accident.

I'm a 15-year-old girl & don't have no father. He died a few yrs. ago & I didn't cry not once. Since then I've hung around rough kids y'know the kind who always get into trouble. Anyway I've never had no respect for anyone 'cept Tim Horton.

I just wanna say this cuz I'll be leavin for a long time soon. Anyway last yr. & this yr. we've gone & mocked out the players after the hockey games. This yr. we started goin to the practices & I finally met Timmy Horton. First I was scared cuz he looked really strong & mean. But we got to talking & I told him I didn't have no father & he told me something I'll never forget. He said:

"Just becuz someone's left the earth doesn't mean they're dead. You're only dead if you're forgotten & not loved. If you still have a place for that person in your heart they're still with you & will never be dead. They've only taken a trip, a long trip. No one can ever be taken away from you if you have faith in them."

I guess I've learned a lot from that. But I never cried as hard as when I heard Horton went on that trip. The thing is Horton may be gone but not dead not really dead & if you ever see good things happening for the Sabres on the ice, that can't really be explained, it can in two words "Tim Horton."

He's with us now he always will & everyone should always believe this.

TIM HORTON

condo in Richmond Hill in 1995 I started going through all of the things I had put away over 20 years earlier. There were a lot of things which had gone unopened for too long. After Tim died, I just couldn't bring myself to look at them.

IN THE DAYS AND MONTHS following Tim's death a lot of nice things were written about Tim as a player, as a friend, as a human being. George Gross remembered his soft-spoken strength, and his inability to say anything nasty about anyone. Paul Rimstead, who'd grown up around the corner from Tim in Sudbury, recalled Tim's reluctance to say anything controversial, and his typical answer to most questions about himself — a shrug and a smile. It was that attitude, according to Rimstead, which best explained the lack of in-depth articles on Tim over the years.

These days Tim is rightly remembered as a throwback; a link between modern hockey and the old approach to the game. But what many people don't realize is that he was a throwback even back then. Rimstead, remembering the trenchcoat and the black oxfords and the thick black-rimmed glasses (the look his teammates dubbed as "Clark Kent"), wrote that when Tim boarded the team bus, "he looked more like a physical education teacher than a tough defenseman in pro hockey. . . . When Horton finally let his hair grow longer it was sort of official to me that the crewcut was gone forever."

185

J. F. (Bunny) Ahearne

Harold E. Ballard

Joseph Cattarinich

**1977
Inductees**

Alex Delvecchio

M.G. (Tim) Horton

ANNUAL INDUCTION DINNER

Toronto   August 25, 1977

The program from
Tim's induction
into the Hockey
Hall of Fame. He
was inducted in
1977, the first year
he was eligible.
The other player
inducted that year
was fellow ironman
and long-time Red
Wings opponent
Alex Delvecchio.
Harold Ballard
was inducted a
a "builder" the
same night.

Punch Imlach gave the dedication speech at
the Hall-of-Fame ceremony. Some of the speeches
at these events can run a little long. My speech
lasted 11 seconds, and I got a standing ovation.

Me and the girls
the night Tim was
inducted into the
Buffalo Sabres
Hall of Fame.

Sergio Mommesso (at the time, the current #7)
presenting a Horton sweater to Kim at the
sweater-raising ceremony in Toronto.
Jeri and Traci look on.

One thing that most of these articles made special note of was Tim's humility. Tim was always reluctant to talk about his accomplishments on the ice with reporters. He was always the last to whoop it up and be photographed in those Stanley Cup years. At home, Tim hated even a photograph of himself in uniform going up on the wall.

A.J. tries his grandfather's sweater on for size at the opening of the Cochrane museum. At six years of age, A.J.'s slapshot was clocked at 45 mph.

Horton and Clancy, the two number 7s, heading for the rafters. Notice the standing ovation. That night was the first time I really knew what it was like for Tim to play in front of all those people.

He'd just laugh and insist that we take it down. I remember one occasion when he took a photo down, tore it up, and wrote, "What do you know?" on the backing where the photo used to be.

And I'm sure he would have been just as uncomfortable with all the attention involved in his Hall-of-Fame induction, which occurred in 1977, the first year he was eligible. But I'm also sure he would have been proud. People had been telling Tim for years that he was headed for the Hall of Fame, but during his last year with the Leafs he got a letter from Connie Smythe telling him he wasn't an honourable person and that he'd do everything in his power to keep him out of the Hall. I responded to that letter myself. Tim and I always got along beautifully with Stafford Smythe, but Connie was a different question entirely.

Tim was inducted with fellow ironman Alex Delvecchio in the Players' category. Harold Ballard, among others, was inducted as a Builder in the same ceremony. I sat next to Ballard on that night; I remember Jean Beliveau was there giving one of the tributes. Tim's tribute was given by Punch

Imlach. These evenings are wonderful for the players and their families, with the one drawback being that the speeches have a tendency of rambling on a little. My speech came late in the evening and lasted 11 seconds; I got a standing ovation. Tim's plaque is up there on the wall with all of his buddies — Bower, Keon, Stanley, Mahovlich, Moore.

Tim's number was honoured twice during the 1995–96 season. The honour was of course long overdue in Toronto, not just for Tim but for King Clancy, who wore the same number. I was down at the Gardens to watch Jim Schoenfeld coach a game recently, and there just aren't enough

Thanking the Buffalo crowd at the sweater-retiring ceremony in 1996. Seymour Knox IV and III are standing behind me. The ceremony was lovely and Darryl Sittler came down from Toronto to present each of my daughters with a replica of Tim's Stanley Cup ring.

The entrance of the Tim Horton Museum in Cochrane, which opened in the summer of 1996. The collection is housed in a railway car at the moment, while they look for a more permanent home. I kind of like it where it is; it's a unique way of presenting an exhibit.

Horton memorabilia at the Tim Horton Museum, a lot of it donated by people of Cochrane. They have things there that even I hadn't seen before.

numbers up there. Dave Keon's sweater should have been up years ago. So should Allan Stanley's, and there are several others. For years the Leafs alumni were completely neglected in Toronto, but after Harold Ballard died and Donald Crump and Cliff Fletcher took over the running of the team, things improved a great deal.

I found out for the first time that evening in Toronto what it was like for Tim to be out on the ice with 20,000 people up there watching. My daughters and I were out at centre ice with King Clancy's sons and two daughters. The two families were presented with a painting and then the two #7 banners were raised slowly to the roof, to a standing

Tim's Hall-of-Fame ring (which Tim Griggs now wears) and his Stanley Cup ring from Toronto.
JOHN SUBURA

ovation. It was a very, very moving moment. The ovation lasted a long time, and on the ice it was just a din, a wall of noise.

A few months later, in January, there was a similarly lovely ceremony in Buffalo when they retired #2, Tim's number with the Sabres. There was a party of about 40 people in the director's lounge with Tim's friends and ex-teammates, and I took my grandsons Tim, A.J., and Corey and my four daughters out on the ice with me for the ceremony. Down in Buffalo, the Leafs also presented each of my four daughters with a replica of Tim's Stanley Cup ring, which I thought was a wonderful gesture.

That same summer, the family and I were also invited up to Tim's home town of Cochrane for the opening of the Tim Horton Museum, a lovely display of sweaters, sticks, photos, and memorabilia which is housed at the moment in a converted railway car near the train yards. There are plans to move the museum to a more permanent home in town, I think, but I'd be just as happy if it stayed where it was. The setting is unique, and appropriate given Tim's connection to the railway while he was growing up. In the summer of 1996, the display was enlarged with a collection of

memorabilia donated by Neil McCullough, one of Jeri's old classmates.

These three events had a lot to do with giving me a sense of closure about Tim's death. I'm not sure I would have started work on this book without them.

Punch Imlach once said that Tim's one weakness as a hockey player was that he was "a peacemaker." On the ice, Tim preferred a bear-hug to a fight, a push to a punch. "He would lean on a player and exhaust him," as Rimstead pointed out.

After talking to Tim's teammates, the thing which strikes you most is the number of them who felt that they were close to him. On any one team he played with, a half a dozen players felt they were as close a friend to Tim as anyone on the team. And they were. Tim always put friends and family ahead of himself — that never changed, not from the day I met him. Everyone was involved, everyone felt important to him — because they were, they *all* were. Jimmy Schoenfeld is right; Tim *was* uncontainable.

We all miss him.

We'll always miss him.

HORTON, TIM

Born Cochrane, Ontario, January 12, 1930
Defence, Shoots right, 5'10" 180 lb.

Regular Season, Playoffs

SEASON	CLUB	LEAGUE	GP	G	A	PTS	PIM	GP	G	A	PTS	PIM
1946–47	Copper Cliff	Senior	9	0	0	0	14	5	0	1	1	0
1947–48	St. Mike's	OHA Jr.	32	6	7	13	137	–	–	–	–	–
1948–49	St. Mike's	OHA Jr.	32	9	18	27	95	–	–	–	–	–
1949–50	Pittsburgh	AHL	60	5	18	23	83	–	–	–	–	–
	Toronto	NHL	1	0	0	0	2	1	0	0	0	2
1950–51	Pittsburgh	AHL	68	8	26	34	129	13	0	0	0	16
1951–52	Pittsburgh	AHL	64	12	19	31	146	11	1	3	4	16
	Toronto	NHL	4	0	0	0	8	–	–	–	–	–
1952–53	Toronto	NHL	70	2	14	16	85	–	–	–	–	–
1953–54	Toronto	NHL	70	7	24	31	94	5	1	1	2	4
1954–55	Toronto	NHL	67	5	9	14	84	–	–	–	–	–
1955–56	Toronto	NHL	35	0	5	5	36	2	0	0	0	4
1956–57	Toronto	NHL	66	6	19	25	72	–	–	–	–	–
1957–58	Toronto	NHL	53	6	20	26	39	–	–	–	–	–
1958–59	Toronto	NHL	70	5	21	26	76	12	0	3	3	16
1959–60	Toronto	NHL	70	3	29	32	69	10	0	1	1	6
1960–61	Toronto	NHL	57	6	15	21	75	6	0	0	0	0
1961–62	Toronto	NHL	70	10	28	38	88	12	3	13	16	16
1962–63	Toronto	NHL	70	6	19	25	69	10	1	3	4	10
1963–64	Toronto	NHL	70	9	20	29	71	14	0	4	4	20
1964–65	Toronto	NHL	70	12	16	28	95	6	0	2	2	13
1965–66	Toronto	NHL	70	6	22	28	76	4	1	0	1	17
1966–67	Toronto	NHL	70	8	17	25	70	12	3	5	8	25
1967–68	Toronto	NHL	69	4	23	27	82	–	–	–	–	–
1968–69	Toronto	NHL	74	11	29	40	107	4	0	0	0	2
1969–70	Toronto	NHL	59	3	19	22	91	–	–	–	–	–
	N.Y. Rangers	NHL	15	1	5	6	16	6	1	1	2	28
1970–71	N.Y. Rangers	NHL	78	2	18	20	57	23	1	4	5	14
1971–72	Pittsburgh	NHL	41	2	9	11	40	4	0	1	1	2
1972–73	Buffalo	NHL	69	1	16	17	56	0	0	1	1	4
1973–74	Buffalo	NHL	55	0	6	6	53	–	–	–	–	–
NHL Totals, 24 seasons			1446	115	403	518	1611	126	11	39	50	183

193

Tim Horton on Playing Defence

Going through Tim's papers, we found a 13-page document written by Tim describing the basics of playing defense. I'm not sure why he wrote it; George Armstrong remembers writing a similar script for a promotional record, but I don't recall Tim doing anything like that. Here's how it looked, and the full, unedited text is transcribed following:

Checking will be done around our own blue line, in our own corners of the rink, and in front of our own net. When checking an opponent, look him in the eye, don't look for the puck. The way that some forwards stickhandle, they can seem to make the puck disappear before your eyes, but if you play the man and not the puck, your checking game will be much more successful. The puck can't go anywhere on its own, so play the puck-carrier.

Bodychecking is a very effective way to stop an opponent. One type of bodycheck is a hip check. A hip check is used when you are skating backwards and the puck-carrier is trying to go around you, and has committed to one side or the other. You swing your hips and hit the puck-carrier at leg level. When bodychecking while skating straight up, hit your opponent with either your chest or your shoulder. This check is the most effective when the opposing player has his head down while carrying the puck. The only fault to bodychecking at the wrong time is that when you commit yourself by moving out toward the incoming forward and you miss him, he has a clear break on your goal. But it is still very important to check the puck-carrier before he comes over your blue line. The longer you can keep the puck-carrier outside your blue line, the less chance they have of scoring on you.

A good back-checking forward can be a great help to you. When one back-checker is coming back on your side and the other wing is open, your defense partner has to play the open wing, so you have to check the centreman carrying the puck. When the other side is covered, your job is reversed with your partner. You have to cover the open wing and your partner checks the puck-carrier. When both opposing forwards are covered by your own back-checking wing men, you and your partner must check the puck-carrier.

We begin by skating backward
from centre ice towards
a corner of the rink as far as
we can, when we are about 15
feet over the blue line the
coach blows his whistle and
at this signal we turn and
skate forwards toward the
corner as hard as we can, stop
quickly and skate forwards
again as fast as possible to
centre ice where we stop and
begin skating backwards
toward the opposite corner
By going to the opposite
corner every second time we
develope our ability at turning
either to our right or left

4 important
sketches or pictures

The one-on-one situation may come up once or twice a game. By this I mean one opposing player carrying the puck toward your goal with you the only defender between him and the goaltender. In this situation you should skate backwards towards your net with your stick extended at arm's length in front of you and with the blade of your stick on the ice. Try to force the puck-carrier

2

checking will be done around our own blue line,
in our own corners of the rink and in front of our
own net. When checking an opponent look him in
the eye, don't look for the puck. The way that
some forwards stickhandle they can seem to make
the puck disappear before your eyes, but if you
play the man and not the puck, your checking
game will be much more successful. The puck
can't go anywhere ~~without it~~ on its own so play
the puck carrier. Bodychecking is ~~a very effective~~ a very effective
way to stop an opponent. ~~Bodycheck is when you~~
~~One type of Bodycheck is a hip check (with your~~
~~hit another player with~~ ~~the~~ ~~one hip~~ ~~you~~
~~hit~~ ~~(when skating middle this check)~~ A hip check is ~~usually used~~
when you are skating backwards and the puck
carrier is trying to go around you, ~~and he~~
~~committed himself to go to one side or the other,~~ you swing your
~~forward and you~~ ~~skate and you~~
hip and hit ~~the~~ the puck carrier ~~around the knees~~ at ~~knee~~ level
~~hit the puck carrier around the knees~~
~~you hip.~~ When bodychecking while ~~skating~~ skating
straight up you hit your opponent with
either your chest or shoulder. This check is the

over towards the side boards or the corner of the rink. Be patient; try to make the puck carrier commit himself and make the first move, but always keep yourself between the puck-carrier and your net. Don't get deked out of position, but try to force the puck-carrier to shoot from a bad angle and your goaltender should be able to stop it.

2 on 1

When faced with a two-on-one situation, and by this I mean two opposing players coming down the ice and you being the only man back to prevent a shot on your goaltender, you have to play the middle of the rink and stay between the two opposing players. The player carrying the puck can do one

9

for the centre of the net. With a hard
low shot you should get your share of goals
and the ones that don't go in will end up
as rebounds and deflections which in turn
are ~~as~~ dangerous ~~as a~~ clear shot on goal.
~~To keep a shot low keep the stick straight & I~~
~~don't flick your wrist~~ use your arms ~~and~~
~~body more than your wrists~~ x The way hockey is
played today the defenseman must be able to
skate as well as the forwards. The day of
the big lumbering defenseman is past. We
have to be able to manouver more than ever
and in this regard I'd like to stress the edge
you may gain by improving your skating
backwards. During our practice sessions ~~we~~
~~we attack~~ we have a ~~great watch~~ ~~practice which~~ special
practice designed to improve our manouver
ility while skating backwards. We start at
centre ice and ~~then~~ skate backwards toward
the corner of the rink. When we are about

(margin notes: shooting, manouverability, skating backwards)

of three things: he can shoot at your net, try to get around you alone, or pass it to his team mate.

Play anticipation

In this situation you must rely on your own sense of play anticipation. By play anticipation I mean that you must know at once what plays the opposing player can possibly make in any given play pattern, you know what plays he can make on you, then try to guess the one he will use and hope you are right. Anticipating a play is a very important part of your defensive game but you can't be right all the time. Just make sure you are not wrong too often.

3 on 1

Should you be the only defenseman back, and there are three opposing players coming down on you, follow the same rule as in the two-on-one situation — back up toward your net with your stick extended at arm's length out in front of you and with the blade on the ice. This is when staying in the centre of the rink and playing the front of your own net is important. It is difficult to prevent a shot on your goal, but try to keep the puck-carrier at a bad angle so that at no time will one of them be clear in front of your own net with the puck. You can't prevent the other team from getting shots on your goal, but you can make these shots easier by keeping the shooter at a difficult angle.

During a hockey game I like to carry the puck. Some defensemen don't, but whether you like to rush with the puck or not, there is one important rule I would like to stress. Always head-man the puck to an open teammate in front of you. One of our big jobs is getting the puck out of our own end of the rink and this can be done easier and faster with a pass than by you carrying it out by yourself.

Another big part of our game is passing the puck. We must learn to lead the man we are passing to, and this can only be done by repeated practice. Try to lay a firm pass far enough ahead of your teammate that he doesn't have to break stride or slow down when he takes it. A good way to improve your passing is to skate up and down the rink with a teammate, all the while passing the puck back and forth to each other. Through this practice you will learn to control the speed of your pass and the speed your teammate is skating.

Blocking shots is another job that is usually left for the defenseman. I find the best way to block shots is to go down on one knee with your stick laying flat on the ice and your free hand also on the ice beside your leg. Try to use every part of your body that's possible to block the shot. This is most effective when you are a distance of 5 to 10 feet away from the shooter; if he is any further away from you when he shoots, it would be easier to catch the puck in your hand. The advantage of going down on one knee and not sprawling on the ice to block the shot is that you can recover quickly if the forward fakes a shot and tries to skate around you.

Shooting

A defenseman should have a good shot, as most of his shots will be from around the blue line. This is the distance on which you should concentrate in practice. Try to keep your shot down — about six inches to a foot off the ice — and aim for the centre of the net. With a hard, low shot you should get your share of goals, and the ones that don't go in will end up as rebounds and deflections which in turn are as dangerous as a clear shot on goal.

10

15 feet inside our blue line the coach blows his whistle and at this signal we turn quickly and skate as hard as we can into the corner of the rink, stop suddenly and skate as hard as we can back to centre ice where we again stop and begin skating backwards toward the corner again as hard as we can. This is repeated, only this time we go to the opposite side and end of the rink. In this way we improve our turning in either direction. Besides being a great physical conditioner, this practice is one of the best for improving your manoeuvrability, which means your ability to change direction quickly while retaining your complete balance. If you have difficulty when you first skate backwards, I think the simplest way to begin would be to lean your body forward slightly, and with your knees slightly bent, put your weight on your toes and lift each skate 2 inches off the ice while you slowly move backwards. As you gain more balance you'll be able to lift your feet higher and soon be skating as well backwards as forwards.

Maneuverability

The way hockey is played today the defenseman must be able to skate as well as the forwards. The day of the big, lumbering defenseman is past. We have to be able to maneuver more than ever, and in this regard I'd like to stress the edge you may gain by improving your skating backwards.

Skating backwards

During our practice sessions we have a special practice designed to improve our maneuverability while skating backwards. We begin by skating backwards from centre ice towards the corner of the rink as fast as we can. When we are about 15 feet over the blue line the coach blows the whistle and at this signal we turn and skate forwards toward the corner as hard as we can, stop quickly, and skate forwards again as fast as possible to centre ice, where we stop and begin skating backwards toward the opposite corner. By going to the opposite corner every second time we develop our ability at turning either to our right or left.

Besides being a great physical conditioner, this practice is one of the best for improving your maneuverability, which means your ability to change directions quickly while retaining your complete balance. If you have difficulty when you first skate backwards, I think the simplest way to begin would be to bend your body forward slightly, and with your knees bent and your weight supported on your toes, lift each skate about two inches of the ice while you slowly move backwards. As you gain more balance you'll be able to lift your feet higher and will soon be skating as well backwards as forwards.

A defenseman's job while killing penalties

A defenseman's job on penalty killing is a little different than during regular play. We play a box-type defense; by this I mean the two forwards play the opposing team's points and the slot, while we defensemen look after the front of the net and our corners. Whenever possible, try to move an opposing player away from the front of your net. He will be trying to block your goaltender's view, or deflect the shot with his stick, or pounce on a rebound, so concentrate on the front of your net and clear away the loose pucks.

Knowing your own players helps also. If I have the puck in the corner or behind our net and am being checked closely so that I can't clear the puck completely out of our end myself, I know that the wing man on my side of the ice will be over on the boards half way between our blue line and the corner. As a result, I can dump the puck up the boards to him and he in turn is able to clear it down the ice, and we are out of trouble.

There are many situations to the game of hockey that can only be covered by playing and practising the game. But I think I have covered the basic and most important ones that will help you improve your playing and also add to your enjoyment while doing so. Playing defense is hard work but it is also a lot of fun, and when you make a good move defensively it can be as heartening as scoring a goal.

I hope you enjoy your hockey as much as I do and don't forget that whenever you are in doubt, stop in at one of our drive-in restaurants and have a delicious hamburger.

Afterword

Four years ago, I carried about a half a dozen boxes out of Lori Horton's basement. Each was filled with newspapers and all kinds of hockey memorabilia from her late husband's career.

Lori and I had agreed that I should look through all of this material so I could learn more about my "Uncle Tim." I had only known him for a short time when I was a kid, and knew very little about his illustrious hockey career. For my part, I agreed to take all of this memorabilia that had been collecting for the past 50 years and turn it into scrapbooks for her grandchildren to look at and enjoy. This is what Lori had intended to do all along, but after Tim's death it was impossible for her to look at all of these letters, pictures, clippings, and family photos without a flood of memories rushing in.

After about a year, I was halfway through my project of creating scrapbooks. I then began showing my work to friends and family. The response from everyone I showed it to was always the same — they said that they knew a lot of people who would also like to see it. It occurred to me then that by publishing a book, we could share all of these memories with everyone.

Another year, and many phone calls later, we had a publisher. We decided that the book should also include personal stories and memories from Tim's friends, teammates, and family should also be included. And everyone we contacted eagerly agreed to sit and talk to us about Tim.

Over the past two years I've met some of the finest, most down-to-earth people you could find, and found out why Tim considered all of these people his friends.

The project turned out to be an immense undertaking, but it was worth every second Lori and I spent on it, because the result, we think, is a fitting tribute to a man we all loved and were proud to have known.

For my part, I'd like to add a special thank-you to my wife Lynette, who spent countless hours helping me put everything together, writing letters, waiting on phone calls, and standing behind me. Her encouragement helped me see this project through.

— *Tim Griggs*